Praise for *Solidarity Ethics*

"Authentic religions are born in a burst of moral energy, stoked by a passion for compassion and justice. If Christianity is sliding into irrelevance it is because fiery prophetic voices like that of Rebecca Todd Peters have not reached into the chilled hearts of those who without moral warrant call themselves Christians."
—Daniel C. Maguire, Marquette University

"*Solidarity Ethics* is a model of Christian feminist social ethics—relational, outward-reaching, global, justice-oriented, and spiritually illuminating."
—Gary Dorrien, Union Theological Seminary

"This morally challenging book by Rebecca Todd Peters should be read by all who are concerned about the gross economic disparities in today's world and what they can do to change them. *Solidarity Ethics* not only provides a compelling treatise on 'solidarity' as a theological and ethical principle but sets forth strategies for how it can be embodied by individuals and communities both here at home and far away."
—Peter Paris, Princeton Theological Seminary

SOLIDARITY ETHICS

SOLIDARITY ETHICS

TRANSFORMATION IN A GLOBALIZED WORLD

REBECCA TODD PETERS

Fortress Press
Minneapolis

Cover design: Rob Dewey

Cover art © Thinkstock

Library of Congress Cataloging-in-Publication Data

Print ISBN: 978-1-4514-6558-7

eBook ISBN: 978-1-4514-6987-5

The paper used in this publication meets the minimum requirements of American National Standard for Information Sciences — Permanence of Paper for Printed Library Materials, ANSI Z329.48-1984.

Manufactured in the U.S.A.

This book was produced using PressBooks.com, and PDF rendering was done by PrinceXML.

this book is dedicated, in solidarity,
to the women and men in the ecumenical movement
who have become my "cloud of witnesses"

CONTENTS

Preface: Seeing with New Eyes

At the age of twenty-four, I attended a young women's leadership development conference in Jamaica sponsored by three international faith-based organizations: the World Council of Churches, the World Student Christian Federation, and the World YWCA. We were a small group of thirty women in our twenties from all parts of the world; many of us were students, but some were also lawyers, ministers, and activists. For ten days, we shared stories of the political realities of our countries and talked about the challenges that women faced in our contexts. We learned about the political and cultural realities of poverty in Jamaica and developed strategies to strengthen our leadership skills. We ate together, swam together, prayed together, and played together—but mostly we talked. We talked about our lives, our experiences, our families, our hopes, and our dreams.

For the first time in my life, I developed relationships with women whose lives were radically different from my own. A woman from Hiroshima shared with us her experience of nuclear weapons as a second-generation survivor of the bomb, and described life for her mother who had lost her legs as a three-year-old in 1945. Women from Sri Lanka, Lebanon, and Liberia told about their experiences living in war-torn countries, and women from Asia spoke passionately about the growing problem of sex tourism, prostitution, and the exploitation of women. Others shared the struggles and challenges that young women face in their contexts, from unwanted pregnancy and access to education to dowries, violence, poverty, and rape.

But it was hearing the story of a young woman named Deysi that has haunted me for years. Late one afternoon, through tears, Deysi shared her experience of the civil war in El Salvador, which had only happened a few years earlier. A death squad had broken into her home and opened fire, killing everyone there—everyone but Deysi. She watched as her brothers and sisters, mother and father were all gunned down in front of her. She had escaped only because she lay still, pretending to be dead. The room was silent while we listened to her words through a translator. Despite having read the stories of the mass killings and unspeakable torture that the death squads had inflicted on the people of El Salvador, I was unprepared for Deysi's words. In the tropical setting of Ocho Rios, where we came together on neutral soil, sharing common meals and teatimes and talking about the call of Christ in the world to challenge social injustice, I was deluded into the perception that as young women, the thirty of us had more in common than we did. Rightly or wrongly, knowing Deysi changed everything. It was because of our common experience, our shared community, because we had broken bread together, because she sat across the room from me and I could look into her eyes, that her story moved me in a way that was different from the stories of people unknown to me.

Over and over again, my experience of national and international social justice work has confirmed that knowing people personally transforms a news story from an item of interest into something personal. Developing relationships with people across lines of difference offers the opportunity to see things differently, through the eyes of another. Given the limitations of our own narrow and specific vantage points, learning how to change our perspective can be an important factor in deepening our understanding of the world around us. Seeing the world through someone else's eyes can help to generate empathy while also contributing to a more nuanced analysis of social problems.

The experience of my first international ecumenical gathering was transformative in another way, involving an encounter on one of the last days while we were telling one another our plans for the future. When I shared that I felt that my calling was to help people, particularly those most marginalized, and that I planned to do this in mission work in the two-thirds world, a young Nigerian lawyer stood and addressed me from across the room. Firmly and resolutely, Sola said, "If you want to help me and my people, the best thing that you can do is to go back to the United States and confront the powers of globalization that are destroying my country and my people." I was caught short; I did not know what to say. Sola's words were an epiphany. As I talked with her later, Sola explained that my social location as a US American gave me a certain privilege of voice and access that she did not have. I could use that privilege responsibly by educating North Americans about the problems of global poverty and injustice and challenging the dominant powers of the International Monetary Fund (IMF) and World Bank, which are headquartered in our nation's capital. Because we had developed a friendship, I was able to hear her words as the challenge of a sister and a friend, rather than as the reproachful words of a stranger. Building community together, studying the Bible, and working on tough issues over a period of ten days challenged us to move beyond pleasantries and ask each other hard questions about where we find God in today's world. God spoke to me through the voice of Sola, calling me to account for my privilege and challenging me to follow the way of Christ in working toward the establishment of peace and social justice in the world.

My encounter in Jamaica was an experience of *metanoia* that opened my eyes to new ways of seeing the world. When I returned to the United States, I brought Sola and Deysi and the other young women I had met with me. They became a cloud of witnesses that helped to reshape my vision and perspective on the global economy and the processes of globalization. Seeing the world with new eyes enabled me to ask questions that had never occurred to me before; questions like: Are there moral limits to corporate profits? Are there moral ceilings and floors that we should place on wages and salaries? Why is it that so many people in our country who work two and three jobs still can't get out of poverty? Why are the products at Walmart so cheap? What is the environmental impact of the food that I buy? Why is it that we have so much and our lives are so comfortable when one-third of the world, or 2.4 billion people, live in poverty?[1] How much is enough, and when does our consumption become morally obscene?

My sense of an appropriate Christian response to poverty was disrupted. Having volunteered over the years at homeless shelters and soup kitchens, I had confused charity with social justice. Furthermore, my desire to move to a distant country and "help" people who were less fortunate than myself, while good-intentioned, served to reinforce two culturally dominant narratives: 1) that poverty is primarily a problem in other, lesser developed countries, and 2) that people in the two-thirds world *need* the help of privileged people from the first world to move out of poverty. The more I researched, the more I realized that these well-intentioned structures of benevolence and charity inevitably contribute to the creation of imbalanced relationships. These relationships allow first-world Christians to feel good about ourselves because we "helped," without ultimately requiring us to change anything about our own personal habits and behaviors or the social and economic structures that shape our societies in patterns of wealth and poverty, have and have-not, deserving and undeserving.

Given the radical economic disparity in our world, discerning how to live with integrity in the midst of systems and structures seemingly outside of our control can generate genuine confusion—if not outright despair—for many first-world people. It is increasingly clear that first-world citizens must radically transform our individual lifestyles while simultaneously working together to change the structures of globalization in our world that privilege the haves at the expense of the have-nots. Developing relationships of solidarity with people across lines of difference—be they differences of race, culture, geography, language, or class—offers a window into new ways of thinking that can help broaden our perspective as well as generate the empathy that is necessary for crafting new strategies to address the root causes of social problems that continue to plague the human family. The ethic of solidarity developed here is intended to offer first-world Christians a new strategy for navigating the morally precarious waters of neoliberal globalization.

Notes

1. World Bank estimates from April 2013, http://web.worldbank.org/WBSITE/ EXTERNAL/TOPICS/EXTPOVERTY/EXTPA/0,,contentMDK:20040961~menuPK:435040~ pagePK:148956~piPK:216618~theSitePK:430367~isCURL:Y,00.html

Acknowledgments

Portions of this book were originally published in the following chapters. I thank the publishers for their permission to use these materials in the current volume.

Excerpts from "Feminist Critical Discourse on Globalization, Economy, Ecology, and Empire," *Ecumenical Review* 64, no. 3 (October 2012): 281–98.

Excerpts from *The Almighty and the Dollar: Reflections on Economic Justice for All*, ed. Mark J. Allman (Winona, MN: Anselm Academic, 2012). Copyright by Anselm Academic 2012. Used by permission of the publisher.

Douglas A. Hicks and Thad Williamson, eds., "Examining the Value of Solidarity as a Moral Foundation for Poverty Alleviation," in *Leadership and Global Justice*, 2012, Palgrave Macmillan reproduced with permission of Palgrave Macmillan. The full published version of this publication is available at: http://us.macmillan.com/leadershipandglobaljustice/DouglasAHicks

"Conflict and Solidarity Ethics: Difficult Conversations on Economics, Religion, and Culture," *College Theology Society Annual* 56 (2011).

"Global Change Context," in *Leading Change in Multiple Contexts: Concepts and Practices in Organizational, Community, Political, Social, and Global Change Settings*, ed. Gill Robinson Hickman (Thousand Oaks, CA: Sage Publications, 2009).

Excerpts from "Assessing the Ethical Landscape of Globalization," in *Ethics in an Era of Globalization*, ed. M.S. Ronald Commers, Wim Vandekerckhove, An Verlinden (London: Ashgate, 2008), 55–72. Copyright © 2008.

"Economic Justice Requires More than the Kindness of Strangers," in *Faith and Economic Life*, ed. Mark Valeri and Douglas A. Hicks (Grand Rapids: Eerdmans, 2008). Reprinted by permission of the publisher; all rights reserved.

"Decolonizing our Minds: Postcolonial Perspectives on the Church," *Women's Voices and Visions of the Church: Reflections from North America*, ed. Letty Russell et al (Geneva: WCC Publications, 2005).

"What Are We to DO: Examining the Moral Challenges of Solidarity for the First World," in *The Grace of Solidarity in a Globalized World*, ed. Mario

DeGiglio-Bellemare and Gabriela Miranda García (Geneva: World Student Christian Federation, 2004).

———

After *In Search of the Good Life* was published in 2004 and I began to speak in different venues about the analysis of globalization that I developed in that book, I was increasingly questioned about what an alternative, justice-oriented vision of globalization might look like in our world. As I travelled around, people often said to me, "This helps me understand the problems associated with globalization, but what do I *do*?" In many ways this book is my response to that familiar question that I have heard over and over again from people in many first-world contexts. I owe a deep debt of gratitude to so many people across the church and the ecumenical movement as well as across the academy who listened to portions of these chapters, challenging my assumptions, asking penetrating questions, and struggling with me to discern how to live differently in the world. My thanks go in particular to the organizers and participants of Young Women's Leadership Development Conference sponsored by World Council of Churches (WCC), World Student Christian Federation (WSCF), and the World Young Women's Christian Association (YWCA) that was held in Jamaica in November of 1991 and to Mary Ann Lundy, Mary Kuhns, Clyde Robinson, the Council on Ecumenical Student Christian Ministries (CESCM), and the WSCF who sent me as a US delegate to a conference that has shaped the direction of my life and my work.

In the years since *In Search of the Good Life* was published, extensive work with the WCC has continued to offer venues for developing the ideas presented in this book and for opportunities to meet and talk with colleagues from around the world about the pressing issues and challenges of globalization. I have been particularly blessed by the support and trust of Robina Winbush, Aruna Gnandason, Martin Robra, Rogate Mshana, Patricia Sheerattan-Bisnauth, and John Gibaut, each of whom have supported my work and my participation in various ecumenical events over the years. The real treasure of these events, for me, is always the conversations, friendships, and solidarity that are built among the participants as we struggle together to work on the presenting issues of wealth, poverty, globalization, and economic and environmental justice. Special thanks to the many participants of the WCC Consultation on "Acting Together for Transformation" and the AGAPE workshop held in Geneva in September 2006; the WCC African Churches' Encounter & African Women's Hearing on Poverty, Wealth and Ecology in Dar Es Salaam, Tanzania, in

November 2007; the World Alliance of Reformed Churches Feminist Dialogue on Economy, Ecology and Empire in Bangalore, India, in August 2008; and the World Council of Churches North American Regional Hearing and Forum on Poverty, Wealth and Ecology in Calgary, Alberta, Canada, in November 2011; and the Faith and Order Standing Commission members with whom I have served for the past seven years. Many of these conversations helped me to think more critically about what solidarity might look like across lines of difference and to think more concretely about the importance of action and accountability. I am also grateful to the organizers of the 2005 and 2006 WCC North American Young Adult Ecumenical Forums who invited me to keynote on issues of globalization and justice and to the young adults who attended and talked with me earnestly and candidly about their hopes and dreams as well as their skepticism and fears. Many of these young people are now leaders in the ecumenical movement, and I am inspired by their on-going passion for justice.

I also had the privilege of presenting ideas from this book as an invited speaker at the Pennsylvania State Pastors Conference sponsored by the Pennsylvania Council of Churches in November 2006; the North Carolina Campus Ministry Retreat in February 2007; Westminster Presbyterian Church in Minneapolis, Minnesota, in September 2007; the Discerning the Signs of the Times conference at Ghost Ranch in July 2010; the US Student Christian Movement conference in April 2013; and as the theologian in residence at New York Avenue Presbyterian Church in Washington, DC in July 2008. In each of these places I was warmly welcomed into conversation with pastors and laypeople who are asking serious questions about how to live faithfully in an increasingly global and unequal world as well as how to lead communities of faith in asking these questions.

In addition to my work in the ecumenical movement and with churches and church people in United States, I have also had incredible opportunities to present my ideas at a variety of academic conferences and events over the past ten years. Portions of these chapters were presented as part of the following major addresses: Founder's Day Address at Elmhurst College in February 2006; Plenary Lecture at the 1st International Global Ethics Conference sponsored by the Center for Ethics and Values Inquiry at Ghent University in Belgium in April 2006; Brueggemann and Kulenkamp Lectures at Eden Theological Seminary in St. Louis in April 2008 (which I shared with Peter Paris); Presidential Address to the American Academy of Religion, Southeast Region in March 2009; Bridgeway Lecture at Furman University in March 2009; Plenary Address to the College Theology Society in Portland, Oregon, in June 2010 (which I shared with Traci West); and keynote address to the *Societas*

Ethicas annual meeting in Frankfurt, Germany, in August 2010. I am grateful to the organizers of these events who invited me to speak and to the feedback and questions that I received from participants. In addition to these invited lectures, portions of the arguments in this book were presented as papers at the following academic conferences: 11th World Congress on Social Economics in Albertville, France, in June 2004; Religion and Social Science section of the American Academy of Religion in San Antonio, Texas, in November 2004; Theological Readings of Economics wildcard session of the American Academy of Religion in San Diego, California, in November 2007; Jepson Colloquium on Leadership and Global Justice at the University of Richmond in January 2011; Catholic Theological Society of America in San Jose, California, in June 2011; and Ethics section of the American Academy of Religion in San Francisco in November 2011. Thanks are due to all those who attended those sessions, engaged my ideas, and shared thoughts and ideas that helped to strengthen the argument in this book.

In addition to the richness that comes with having one's ideas engaged in the public sphere, much of the work of a scholar is enabled by the amazing resources afforded to us by being members of institutions of higher education. I am deeply fortunate to be at an institution that values scholarship and teaching—the two passions of my professional life! Elon University supported this work through a sabbatical leave during the 2007–2008 academic year as well as through course releases that have supported my research in significant ways over the years. Elon has also been generous in their support of my professional development and have funded travel to more conferences than I can count. But Elon is more than an institution. It is made up of real people who are good colleagues and dear friends. There are so many people at Elon who make my life richer and more complete, but I would be remiss if I did not thank the following people for their on-going support and encouragement over the years, including administrators Steven House, Leo Lambert, Maurice Levesque, Alison Morrison-Shetlar, and Tim Peeples; my departmental colleagues Amy Allocco, Geoff Claussen, Lynn Huber, Jim Pace, Michael Pregill, Jeffrey Pugh, L.D. Russell, and Pamela Winfield; and all my colleagues on the Faculty Research and Development committees over the years who not only supported my scholarship through funding but also awarded me the 2012 Distinguished Scholar Award, the highest award for scholarship on Elon's campus. Thanks are also due to my Theology from the Margins (2010), Feminist Theologies (2013), and Wealth and Poverty (2012, 2013) classes, who all read drafts of this book and offered their feedback. In particular, I thank Charlie Loeser, Kiva Nice-Webb, and Will Brummett, who asked penetrating questions and helped me see the text from a different perspective, and Caitlin Goodspeed, whose interviews with Grace Hackney and Fred Bahnson informed chapter 5. Special thanks are also due to Rachel Zimmerman and Sarah Holland for help with the bibliography and the permissions.

Another benefit and privilege of being a scholar is the opportunity to develop personal and professional relationships with colleagues that are nurtured in person at sporadic conferences, meetings, and events but that are truly sustained through our on-going virtual dialogue and support. Given the busyness of life, there are many dear friends and colleagues who have shared their time generously with me over the years to read and offer feedback on various drafts of chapters, lectures, and even whole book manuscripts. My deepest thanks are due to Laura Stivers, Doug Hicks, Mary Hobgood, Henry Carrigan, Gary Dorrien, and Nicole Murphy,

who have each read all or part of this manuscript and offered substantive feedback that has helped to improve the quality of my writing and my argument. Others were dialogue partners at conferences or events where I presented my ideas, and my conversations with them have significantly influenced the development of my thought; these dialogue partners include Gloria Albrecht, Peter Paris, Traci West, John Shelley, Puleng LenkaBula, Chris Lind, Nancy Cardoso Pereira, Carol Robb, Omega Bula, Fulata Moyo, Damayanthi Niles, Sue Davies, Athena Peralta, Mai Ki, Elizabeth Hinson-Hasty, and Edie Rasell. The friendship and professional support I have enjoyed over the years from Elizabeth Bounds, Michael Bourgeois, Pamela Brubaker, Marvin Ellison, Marilyn Legge, Dan Spencer, and Randy Styers has been invaluable for my sanity and my career. The willingness to hang out late into the night in obscure hotel rooms, drink wine, and laugh until we cry is another measure of friendship and support among colleagues and, in addition to many of those named above, I thank Jen Ayres, Kate Blanchard, Gay Byron, Letitia Campbell, Monica Coleman, Melanie Harris, Jennifer Harvey, Grace Kao, Grace Kim, Cynthia Moe-Lobeda, Kate Ott, Garland Pierce, Melissa Snarr, and Aana Vigen for their support.

The production of a book takes many hands, and I have appreciated the many people I have worked with at Fortress Press, including Michael Gibson, Lisa Gruenisen, Marissa Wold, and Elliot Ritzema, as well as Karen Schmitt who prepared the index.

In addition to the community of colleagues who support me professionally, I am ceaselessly grateful for love and support of my closest family and friends. To the daycare families who continue to share meals and outings—Patti and Bill, Tana and John, Holly and Tommy, Matina and Olav; to our Elon friends with whom I share more than work—Brooke and Tom, Cindy and Richard, Ann and Neil; and to my dearest friends Kris and Dave and their boys, Will and John, I offer my thanks for your care of my family and me and for sharing your lives with us. To my mother, there are no thanks large enough for all that you have done and continue to do to nurture my family and me. The reality of working families is that we cannot do it all by ourselves, and you have stepped in on countless occasions at the drop of a hat to help us fill in the gaps. More importantly, your presence enriches our lives on a daily basis, and we are very thankful you are a significant part of our lives.

Finally, to my husband Jeff and our daughters, Sophie and Eve—to you I owe the deepest gratitude. Your support of my work touches me to my soul. Your understanding of the way in which my calling to live faithfully often takes me away from home and across the world and your recognition that this is what not only makes me who I am but enables me to be the best mother and partner I can be is truly remarkable. Thank you for loving me for who I am and encouraging and supporting me along the way.

As I struggle with the moral question of my own global footprint as a Christian ethicist and theologian who genuinely seeks radical transformation of the global economic structures that are destroying our world, I do not know whether the personal choices I am making to travel and engage in dialogue, debate, and strategizing for social change are the right choices. I do know that each person that I meet, each conversation that I have about these issues, and each trip that I make contributes to developing my thoughts and ideas more fully, and I am deeply grateful to all of the people who joined me in this conversation and invited me into theirs. My work and my life is all the richer for it.

Introduction: The Problem of Globalization

Living as a first-world citizen in a globalizing world presents a great moral challenge. Many people are aware that the wealthiest 20 percent of the world's population consume 76.6 percent of the world's resources, while the world's poorest 20 percent are left with 1.5 percent.[1] However, fewer people are aware that while basic education for everyone in the world would cost six billion dollars, US Americans spend eight billion dollars annually on cosmetics; that while water and sanitation for everyone in the world would cost nine billion dollars, Europeans annually spend eleven billion dollars on ice cream; that while providing reproductive health care for all women in the world would cost twelve billion dollars, together US Americans and Europeans currently spend that much annually on perfumes; that while basic health and nutrition for everyone in the world would only cost thirteen billion dollars, Europeans and US Americans spend seventeen billion dollars annually on pet food.[2] These facts offer a glimpse into the different social realities of life in the global North and the global South.

Certainly there is nothing morally questionable about eating ice cream, wearing perfume, or having a pet. Yet these statistics do portray a troubling moral crisis in our world. How is it possible that so few have so much, when so many have so little? Obviously, the money currently being spent on personal consumption reflected in these figures cannot simply be shifted to cover expenditures like basic education or water and sanitation for the world's population. Our global economic system and its disparities are not that simple. There is something more deeply amiss in our world that we must try to comprehend.

The underlying moral problem that these statistics reveal is twofold. First, these statistics demonstrate a behavioral problem on the part of people living in the first world that manifests itself as relative indulgence and overconsumption by the world's elite in the face of human suffering around the world.[3] Second, these massive inequalities between life in the first world and life in the two-thirds world reveal an underlying structural problem in our global society: that the contemporary structures of the global economy—including neoclassical economic theory, international financial institutions, global trade agreements, and the actions of transnational business corporations—are designed by people in the first world in ways that disproportionately benefit those of us living in the first world. The wealthy elite, namely the people who live in the first world and their elite compatriots in developing countries (who are often educated in the first world), are the architects of the global economic and political structures that shape the face of globalization and global economic policy. While it is essential for individual first-world consumers to recognize our complicity in perpetuating this global system of increasing inequality, it is also vital that we recognize the systemic root of the problems that are reflected in these statistics. These two factors—personal complicity and behavior alongside structural analysis and accountability—are the foundations for changing the direction of our global future.

An ethic of solidarity is both a model for first-world Christians for how to live faithfully in the midst of a globalizing world (personal complicity and behavior) as well as a framework for a new way of imagining our political economy and our social networks and interactions (structural analysis and accountability).[4] An ethic of solidarity is a transformative ethic, rooted in the principles of sustainability and social justice, that requires first-world citizens to work simultaneously on transforming personal habits and lifestyles as well as global economic and political structures that perpetuate inequality and injustice. The starting point for this project is the problem of social injustice that is generated by the dominant form of globalization in our world and the economic ideology that undergirds it.[5] In these pages, I will explore the richness, depth, and challenge that a theology of solidarity offers as the foundation for economic and social relationships as opposed to the guiding principles of individualism, profit, and wealth accumulation that currently drive the economic structures of human society.

My work as a Christian social ethicist is best defined as feminist liberation ethics, a strand of thought rooted in the tradition of social Christianity that takes the problem of social injustice as its starting point.[6] The tradition of Christian social ethics is the branch of ethical inquiry that understands its task as "the relentless advocacy of ethical positions on matters of public policy based on Christian theological criteria."[7] By its nature, Christian social ethics is public theology that engages in critical social analysis with an eye toward developing normative moral criteria to help shape human behavior and social policy. Critical feminist theologies also shape the methodological perspective of this study in several significant ways, including the emphasis on examining interstructured oppression, privileging standpoint theory and the importance of social location, and the emphasis on developing relationships across lines of difference that is foundational to the ethic of solidarity developed here.

Assessing the Morality of Economic Globalization

Economies and markets are social structures created by human beings. They are the means by which people order and structure the basic activities of human existence. The economies, markets, and social systems that humans create are moral structures that reflect particular values expressing particular understandings of what it means to be human and what it means to live a good life. As such, it is important to interrogate the moral codes and priorities that are embedded in economic systems to ensure that these systems reflect the values that societies hold most dear. The current economic order, which is commonly referred to as "neoliberal globalization," is a complex idea that deserves some analysis.

The term "globalization" is currently used in a wide variety of ways. Generally speaking, it refers to economic, social, political, and cultural processes that serve to break down traditional barriers that have separated peoples, nations, and cultures from one another. To the extent that globalization refers to interaction between cultures, trade partnerships and agreements, migration, and technology transfer, it is hardly a new phenomenon. Just as surely as tribal and cultural identity can be traced to the evolution of *homo sapiens* as a species, the interaction, intermarriage, and trading relationships between different clans and tribes represent the earliest patterns of commerce and social interaction between groups that defined themselves as somehow different from one another. These behaviors and interactions mark the history of human civilization over the millennia. Sometimes cultural interaction has progressed peacefully and functioned in mutually beneficial ways; at other times nations have acted as aggressors against their neighbors or against those peoples and cultures that they perceived to be inferior.

The political and economic shifts that accompanied the end of the Second World War led to the rise of a new geopolitical landscape that included two major changes. The first change was the solidification of the Western and Eastern political "blocs" that came to be known respectively as the "first" and the "second" world. The second change was a growing concern with the economic development of newly independent nations in Africa, Latin America, and to a lesser extent, Asia. The working assumption of the Western countries, or the first world, was that these former colonies needed to develop their assets and resources in ways that would make them more prosperous. The general consensus was that the best way for them to succeed was to emulate the industrial development model that had propelled the first world to economic success. These countries were referred to as "underdeveloped" or "developing." They also came to be known as the "third world," and more recently, the "two-thirds world" or the "Global South."

The most significant changes that have shaped the global economy and the context of globalization in which we now live took shape in the 1980s. At that time, a new set of economic policies were promoted by leading politicians in Britain and the United States that have come to be characterized by the label "neoliberal."[8] These policies brought business and political leaders together in the task of developing a more integrated global economy. The guiding principle behind these policies was that economic growth and the health of the economy were best achieved by creating political environments that allowed "market mechanisms" to function freely without government interference. Also referred to by the names "supply-side economics," "Washington Consensus," "laissez-faire," and the "free market," these economic approaches relied heavily on deregulation, privatization, and increasing international trade, and were heavily promoted by the administrations of Margaret Thatcher and Ronald Reagan.

With the disintegration of the former Soviet Bloc countries in the last decades of the twentieth century, economists and politicians heralded the triumph of capitalism and sought to extend neoliberal policies around the world in an effort to create a single, unified global market that functioned with a common set of economic principles and assumptions. While various engines of the global economy, like the International Monetary Fund (IMF), the World Bank, and the World Trade Organization (WTO), had already moved toward neoliberal policies in the early 1980s, by the end of the decade these dominant international financial institutions promoted neoliberal ideas as the foundational economic assumptions of their models of development. The economic power that these institutions wielded, through economic policies and critically important credit ratings of developing countries' economies, allowed them to pressure many developing countries to conform to Western economic assumptions about growth and trade. These assumptions often discounted the particular circumstances, histories, and cultural specificities of individual countries and their economies.[9] The structural adjustment policies that accompanied the neoliberal model functioned to eviscerate social spending on education, health, unemployment, and other social services in countries where many people were unable to compensate for this loss of government services. These cutbacks had significant impacts on literacy rates, prenatal care, infant mortality, and the general health and well being of many people living in or near poverty.[10]

As a nation, the United States is deeply invested in the promotion and continuation of the neoliberal model of globalization. From our fourteen-trillion-dollar debt to the military-industrial complex that accounts for 45 percent of our national budget, US Americans have structured our economy in ways that are beholden to a neoliberal economic agenda. The allure of an ideology that recognizes the capitalist, consumerist, and individualist way of life as the pinnacle of civilization, and a capitalist market economy as superior to all others, has structured our lives and our minds in particular ways. Unfortunately, privilege and wealth are too often accompanied by a complacency that blinds us to our own weaknesses. As a country, we have become a people that are largely ignorant of the economic institutions of globalization like the IMF, World Bank, and the WTO. Many people in the United States do not know what these institutions do or how they function, but ignorance does not reduce the moral culpability of US Americans for the actions of their government working through these institutions. The very presence of the World Bank and IMF in Washington, DC tells volumes about the influence and control that the United States has in shaping their policy directives.[11]

In this book, the term "economic globalization" is used to refer specifically to the form of globalization that is driven by neoliberal economic theories and activities promoted by US economists, business people, and public officials. While many US Americans have benefited handsomely from neoliberal globalization through wealth gained from financial investment and transactions to inexpensive food, clothes, and electronics, the neoliberal global order has also had a negative impact on the lives of many people living in this country. The growing gap between the rich and the poor that has increased dramatically since the 1990s, the realities of outsourcing and free trade that have contributed to the continued loss of working-class industrial jobs, the subprime lending crisis, and the shifting of the tax burden from the wealthy to the working poor are all consequences of a rise of neoliberal culture that is increasingly shaping the political–economic landscape in the US.[12] These negative consequences of economic globalization help make it easier for US Americans to see the ways in which the neoliberal agenda that has been exploiting the developing world for decades has also been slowly undermining the capacity of people across the economic spectrum to create a "good life" here at home.

Neoliberal globalization is a particular ideology, or belief system, that offers humankind one pathway for organizing economic behavior and transactions. It is not, however, the only model of how international and domestic economic arrangements could be ordered. When viewed from the perspective of the poor and disenfranchised, the morality of neoliberal globalization is far from benign. In fact, the current form of neoliberal globalization mimics the patterns of colonialism and exploitation that dominated international affairs for the last several hundred years. While it purports to be the only way to end poverty, it often functions to impoverish people, communities, and cultures through the implementation of free-market solutions and theories that build up the wealth and power of the world's most powerful economic and political players.[13] Unfortunately, the univocal focus on free-market solutions to poverty draws on Western, neoclassical economic assumptions about human behavior, desire, values, and social reality that do not necessarily correspond to the social reality of the twenty-first century. By focusing almost exclusively on promoting macroeconomic policies to generate economic growth through free-trade zones, growing crops for export, and pushing integration of developing world economies into the global economy, the capitalist approach to addressing poverty fails to allow proponents of neoliberalism to pay adequate attention to the complex factors that contribute to poverty or to the unique forms that poverty takes in different cultural contexts.

Neoliberal policies have certainly functioned to create wealth. The moral question, though, is, "Who has this wealth benefited?" From a Christian ethical perspective, drawing on the deep traditions of justice and care of neighbor as the ethical cornerstones of reflection, a more trenchant moral question is, "What effect do these policies have on the poor and the most marginalized people in society?" Valuing the perspectives of the poor and marginalized allows for engagement in a process of critical social analysis that highlights the processes of globalization from a different perspective than the dominant vision of privilege that accompanies much discourse on globalization in the first world. The current economic crisis offers an opportunity to open up a whole new discussion on political economy that has the potential to move beyond the twentieth-century debates over individualism vs. collectivism. Despite the globally integrated and interconnected world of the twenty-first century, no single master narrative of economic transactions, development, or prosperity is possible or even advantageous in a world that is as diverse and economically uneven as the present world. In considering the moral underpinnings of globalization and economic exchange, it is necessary to examine what values undergird different visions and interpretations of globalization and to expose the ways in which all forms of globalization are not morally equivalent.

The current model of neoliberal globalization is not the only way to shape globalization processes in our world. Global warming and climate change are teaching us that economic integration is too narrow a lens through which to think about the relationships of a global community. Because we share a single ecological space, the habits and practices of people in different parts of the world are leading us toward a new consciousness in which we are forced to recognize the radical interdependence that we share as life forms in a finite space. This new consciousness marks a radical shift between the social and economic worlds of eighteenth-century Europe, where capitalism developed, and the realities of life in the twenty-first century.

Adam Smith and David Ricardo, two of the "fathers" of modern economic theory, did not live in an industrial world with airplanes, high-speed tanker travel, the Internet, and a looming climate change crisis. Their theories of self-interest and comparative advantage belong to a different social and political world that simply does not translate adequately into our own. The philosophical revelations of the Enlightenment that individuality and human rights ought to be the foundation of human society were significant milestones in human development in the 1700s, and these ideas have led to enormous strides forward for the civil rights of minorities and women in many contexts. It is true that all peoples or governments around the world do not necessarily share these assumptions that are taken for granted by Western democracies. For this reason, it is essential to retain an affirmation of the importance of individual self-worth and dignity as important foundational aspects of understanding human nature. At the same time, an overemphasis on individual rights has eclipsed our understanding of the common good. In some cases, where Western values have heavily influenced economic policy, an emphasis on the rights of individuals (for profit or private ownership) has forced communities in the developing world to conform to Western norms of individualism at the expense of their ability to recognize and affirm the value of interdependence. What is at stake for the health and well-being of people and the planet is the ability of Western nations and their leaders to hold the values of individual rights and private property alongside the values of interdependence and sustainability in ways that will shape the practice of globalization in new directions. As a moral philosopher, Smith rooted his economic theories in a moral framework that assumed compassion; he would hardly recognize the economic theory of today that claims to stand outside of morality.[14]

By contrast, a theology of solidarity is firmly rooted in the values of mutuality, justice, and sustainability. Solidarity is a meaningful response for first-world Christians to the environmental degradation, economic disparity, and unjust form of globalization that plague our world today. It requires recognition of the disparity between the dominant, self-centered norms of economic globalization that currently shape economic discourse and practice in our society and the need for moral norms that guide economic interactions in ways that promote the common good. In a world that values and promotes unmitigated consumerism and wealth creation, practicing an ethic of solidarity requires first-world citizens to think and act in countercultural ways.

A Tale of Two Fires

The heart of the moral question that first-world citizens must answer in facing neoliberal globalization is this: to what extent will one participate in a system that benefits some at the expense of others? Furthermore, to what extent are one's own daily habits and practices complicit in the exploitation of other human beings and the planet? These are the questions that shape the present inquiry. A comparison of two industrial fires can help to frame the problem.

In May of 1993, in what has been called "the worst industrial fire in the history of capitalism,"[15] hundreds of low-wage factory workers were trapped inside a burning toy factory on the outskirts of Bangkok, Thailand. Official reports listed the dead at 188 and the injured at 469. Survivors reported that the main doors were locked and windows had been blocked to prevent pilfering. Stuffing and animal fibers used to make the toys had littered the factory. Furthermore, while Thai law requires that the fire-escape stairways of such a large factory be sixteen to thirty-three feet wide, this factory's were a mere four-and-a-half feet wide, and cheap construction allowed steel girders and stairways to crumple easily in the heat.

While the tragic fire at the Kader Industrial Toy Company happened in Thailand, a deeper examination of the circumstances reveals a bit of the complex web of global economic integration and some of the moral problems associated with it. The Kader factory had contracts with Toys R Us, Fisher-Price, Hasbro, Tyco, Arco, Kenner, Gund and J. C. Penney for whom they manufactured Bugs Bunny, Bart Simpson, and Sesame Street toys destined for export to US American consumers. This factory was one of many that have sprung up in the developing world in recent decades, often accompanied by low wages and poor working conditions and made more attractive for investors due to lax environmental laws and government oversight. The Kader fire is a prime example; shoddy construction, failure to follow legal safety codes, dangerous inattention to the storage of flammable materials, and carelessness regarding fire safety procedures all contributed to the fire—and were well within the arena of human control.

Before this tragedy, the Triangle Shirtwaist Company fire of 1911 in New York City had ranked as the worst industrial fire in history. The Triangle fire became legendary and ushered in a new era of regulatory protection for US American workers. In fact, the outrage of citizens over the fire was so pronounced that hundreds of thousands of New Yorkers showed up for the funeral procession of the six unidentified victims in a driving rain.[16] The New York state legislature set up an investigative committee that led to the modernization of the state's labor laws. It is certainly true that working conditions had been poor in factories throughout the nineteenth century as the era of industrialization firmly took root in the United States and Europe. However, labor organizers, concerned citizens, and Christians active in the social gospel movement all collaborated to rectify working conditions and bring about statutory reform that protected workers from exploitation and abuse.[17]

In sharp contrast to the moral indignation that followed the Triangle fire, the Bangkok fire was barely noticed by those outside of Thailand, primarily eliciting moral indifference from the world's elite. Today, similar tragedies continue to be commonplace in the low-wage factories, processing plants, and agriculture jobs that fuel the growth of the global economy by providing consumers with inexpensive goods and services and investors with remarkable profits.

The preventable nature of the fire at Kader combined with the fact that it was a factory producing goods for export to the United States (and other Western consumers) raises complicated questions about moral responsibility. Most US American consumers have bought a toy from one of these companies in their lifetime, and most of those people probably gave no thought to where the toy came from. The fact is, first-world consumers make too many purchases every day to stop and think about where each product originated: who grew our food, whose hands assembled our electronics, whose lives were risked in the manufacture of our toys.

Martin Luther King Jr. believed that the greatest tragedy of his era was the "appalling silence of the good people."[18] Unfortunately, the current era is also marked by much silence on the part of many "good people." While some people who are made aware of egregious human rights violations respond with moral outrage, too many of the good people who remain silent fail to see their own connection to the crises of our world. Others lack a vision of how to respond, even if they are motivated by a desire to help. There are, of course, many people in the first world who respond with outrage to exposés in the daily media. This kind of consumer response can be useful in addressing the immediate problem of child labor, unpaid wages, or unsafe working conditions in a particular factory or manufacturing line (remember the Kathie Lee Gifford and Nike scandals related to sweatshop labor?). But campaigns like these only address the presenting problems and lack a deeper understanding of the complexity of issues of free trade, global economics, and social injustice. Without such understanding, these actions and campaigns are not likely to contribute to long-term solutions. An ethic of solidarity offers a vision of how to respond to the crises that face the human community by developing relationships of mutuality and justice and learning how to see social problems in new ways that allow for the development of new models and structures for economic exchange that promote the common good.

FOUNDATIONS FOR AN ETHIC OF SOLIDARITY

Solidarity is the building of relationships between people across lines of difference with the explicit or implicit intention of working together for social change. Relationships of solidarity are rooted in the mutual recognition of the human dignity that everyone possesses and that Christians understand as a reflection of the *imago Dei*. While these relationships may be transitory or long-lasting, they are substantive and represent a long-term commitment to the shared principle of a just social order that cares for both people and the planet. There are three key points that are foundational for first-world people who wish to develop an ethic of solidarity:

1) Understanding social location and personal privilege

2) Building relationships with people across lines of difference

3) Engaging in structural change

First, our social location in the world is an important factor in how we understand and interpret the world. The term "social location" refers to that set of identity-forming circumstances, like race, gender, ethnicity, culture, sexual orientation, and class that affect and influence one's experience of the world. Social location, life experience, education, training, faith commitments, and theological influences all work together to shape people's worldview, and all of these factors significantly shape the *doing* of theology and ethics in our world. How we understand and think about God, the sacred, and what it means to live faithfully in the world are all shaped by who we are. Given the hegemonic role that first-world countries have played in shaping the engines of globalization, and given our current political and economic power in the world, understanding the privileges that accrue to first-world people vis-à-vis the people who have been socially, politically, and economically marginalized by current globalization practices will be an essential aspect of this inquiry. Examining a social problem by asking questions about how the privileges of race, class, and gender shape the social reality is one aspect of engaging in critical social theory, which is an essential foundation of Christian social ethics.[19]

Second, developing relationships with people across lines of difference is essential to promoting consciousness-raising and sustaining long-term social change. Philosopher Kwame Appiah argues that experiences of cultural difference do more to open our minds to difference than reading or learning about difference.[20] For most readers of this book, immediate and personal contact with social injustice comes in the form of encountering people who are oppressed. If these encounters lead to more long-term relationships and partnerships between individuals or communities of people, they can be an essential aspect of an ethic of solidarity. Developing significant personal relationships with real people offers the possibility of changing the way we understand the world. These relationships can help us think about the world through the eyes of others. "The poor" are no longer statistics on a page, but living, breathing people with stories, families, hopes, and dreams.

While crossing the many barriers of ethnicity, class, race, education, and nationality that separate people from one another may not necessarily make them friends, what it can do is to help Christians understand Jesus' gospel call to love their neighbor in a new way. Jesus does not tell people that they must make their neighbor into a friend, but rather his admonition is to recognize the common humanity that binds people together and to affirm that all people deserve to be treated with love, compassion, and equality. While experiential education and practices of immersion run the risk of voyeurism and exploitation of marginalized people, if these experiences are planned with the participation of local participants and as part of a larger examination of social and structural injustice, they can be an important factor in working toward social transformation.[21]

Third, successful long-term social change requires addressing the structural root of social problems and injustice. Sociologist Robert Wuthnow reports that two-thirds of the members of religious communities say their congregation is involved in operating a soup kitchen or food program.[22] Likewise, often when people see others on the street who are hungry and homeless, an immediate and compassionate response is to reach out to them and feed and shelter them. However, in today's world many of the people who are poor, marginalized, or abused by the economic and environmental excesses of neoliberal globalization do not need charity—what they need is justice. While there is certainly a place for the work of charity, an ethic of solidarity focuses on the essential work of social justice as a necessary factor in changing the direction of our world toward a more just and peaceful community.

For many people, religious communities and belief systems serve as the primary source for moral education, including beliefs about human nature, right and wrong, and justice and injustice. While there are certainly people who derive their moral sensibilities from other locations (e.g., philosophy, humanism), the role of religion in shaping the moral sensibilities of the world's people is still formidable. In addressing issues of conflict and social injustice in the world, it is important to recognize the significant role that religion plays in shaping people's worldviews and moral ideals. Embracing religious traditions and communities as significant partners in the work of conflict transformation and social justice is an essential element of working toward positive social change in our world.

The task of discerning how Christians are to live faithfully in the world is the fundamental concern of Christian ethics. While timeless principles like love and justice are recognized as transcending any particular time period (and any particular religious tradition), how followers are to live out these principles is not always immediately evident. Knowing how to "do justice" requires people to identify and challenge the injustices that are prevalent in society. Beverly Harrison has described the intellectual work of theology as one of "reappropriating all our social relations, including our relations to God, so that shared action toward genuine human and cosmic fulfillment occurs."[23]

Engaging in this kind of theological work requires people to reclaim control of their social relations and recreate the structures of society in ways that are consistent with the biblical lessons of how to live a just and faithful life. This is where Christian social ethics begins, with an understanding that the call of Micah and the prophets to a life of justice, love, and humility before God is also the call to follow Christ in the world. By its very nature, Christian social ethics is public theology that engages in critical social analysis with an eye toward developing normative moral criteria to help shape human behavior and social policy. From this perspective, the task of Christian ethics becomes one of social transformation and social change.

CONCLUSION

It is clear that the planet is not able to sustain a global population that desires to live as first-world citizens currently live. Even more importantly, there is little evidence that first-world lifestyles that revolve around money, consumer goods, and entertainment have improved the happiness of first-world people.

Certainly, it is true that developments over the last hundred years like antibiotics, vaccines, and access to clean water have reduced infant mortality and generally increased the health and well-being of many people living in the developed world. Likewise, labor-saving devices like refrigerators, washing machines, and running water have certainly transformed women's lives and family life in general, easing the daily workload in the home. None of the advances that have been made in medicine, science, and technological innovation should be minimized, nor should the pre-industrial past be romanticized. However, a number of significant lifestyle shifts that have accompanied industrialization have increased humanity's environmental footprint with questionable contributions to the overall well-being of our lives as a community of citizens or a community of nations. Changes that have transformed the lives of those in the first world in recent decades must be examined not just on a personal level but also on a social level. What impact do these changes have on families and communities of people living halfway around the world, and on future generations?

A different world is possible. A different form of globalization and a world order marked by social justice and sustainability are possible. The economic crisis that has heralded the beginning of the twenty-first century requires new social narratives, new ways of being in the world, and a new ethic that offers us a pathway toward achieving this goal. An ethic of solidarity offers just such a pathway.

Notes

1. The World Bank, *World Development Indicators, 2008* (Washington DC: Development Data Group, 2008).

2. United Nations Development Programme, "Chapter 1," in *The Human Development Report*, 1998, http://hdr.undp.org/en/reports/global/hdr1998.

3. Thomas Princen, "Consumption and its Externalities: Where Economy Meets Ecology," in *Confronting Consumption*, ed. Thomas Princen, Michael Maniates, and Ken Conca (Boston: MIT Press, 2002), 23–42. Princen defines overconsumption as the aggregate effect of consumptive behavior of individuals that actually functions to undermine a species's life-support system. While Princen's interest is primarily in the aggregate environmental effects of individual consumer behavior, his concept is instructive here as a way of understanding how individual consumer behavior that seems reasonable and appropriate has an aggregate negative effect on the well-being of the human species as a whole.

4. Certainly, there are many people in the United States and other first-world countries who struggle against economic injustice and poverty on a daily basis. I do not intend to imply that *all* people living in the first world are wealthy. Nevertheless, many of the economic advantages of neoliberal economic globalization impact the relative quality of life of people living in or near poverty in the first world vis-à-vis their neighbors in the global south. While there are many fine works that address the important issues of poverty in the United States and the first world, this

book is intended to ask particular questions about the ethical and moral status and responsibility of people with privilege who are complicit in or benefit from the current form of neoliberal globalization that dominates the global political economy. Furthermore, since the book is written from a US American perspective of privilege, it often uses examples from that context. Given the fact that some of the challenges of lifestyle, environmental impact, complicity of supporting dominant forms of globalization and struggles to work toward structural change are shared more widely by people who live in the first world, I often speak more broadly for what an ethic of solidarity might mean for "first-world Christians" or "first-world people." Readers can decide for themselves whether they are implicated in the analysis presented.

5. In my first book (*In Search of the Good Life: The Ethics of Globalization* [New York: Continuum, 2004]), I offered a detailed ethical analysis of four different models of globalization (neoliberal, development, earthist and postcolonial) as a way of helping people understand that how we globalize the world is a choice that people are making and that different models of globalization embody different moral visions of "the good life." This book assumes much of the critique of the different models of globalization presented in that book and develops an ethic of solidarity as a normative Christian ethical response to the inadequacies of the dominant forms of globalization prevalent in the contemporary world.

6. Gary Dorrien offers a historical analysis of social Christianity in his book *Soul in Society: The Making and Renewal of Social Christianity* (Minneapolis: Fortress, 1995). For discussion of feminist ethics see Lois K. Daly, ed., *Feminist Theological Ethics: A Reader*, Louisville: Westminster John Knox, 1994, esp. chs. 1–2.

7. Joseph C. Hough Jr., "Christian Social Ethics as Advocacy," *Journal of Religious Ethics* 5, no. 1 (1977): 123. June O'Connor's essay, "On Doing Religious Ethics," in *Women's Consciousness, Women's Conscience*, ed. Barbara Hilkert Andolsen, Christine E. Gudorf, and Mary D. Pellauer (Minneapolis: Winston, 1985), is also a good introduction to the tasks of religious ethics. She describes these tasks as not only the decisions and actions that one takes in response to moral questions, but also attention to the interpretive framework or worldview that shapes one's decisions and actions and the epistemological perspective that shapes one's worldview.

8. David Harvey, *A Brief History of Neoliberalism* (New York: Oxford University Press, 2005).

9. Joseph E. Stiglitz, *Globalization and Its Discontents* (New York: W.W. Norton, 2002).

10. Pamela Sparr, ed., *Mortgaging Women's Lives: Feminist Critiques of Structural Adjustment* (London: Zed Books, 1994).

11. For more detailed information about the history and actions of the World Bank and IMF, see Catherine Caufield, *Masters of Illusion: The World Bank and Poverty of Nations* (New York: Henry Holt and Company, 1996) and Bruce Rich, *Mortgaging the Earth: The World Bank, Environmental Impoverishment, and the Crisis of Development* (Boston: Beacon, 1994).

12. Patricia Ventura, *Neoliberal Culture: Living with American Neoliberalism* (London: Ashgate, 2012).

13. Jeffrey D. Sachs's book, *The End of Poverty: Economic Possibilities for Our Time* (New York: Penguin, 2005), proposes an economic "ladder" that poor countries can use to climb out of poverty.

14. For a more detailed discussion of Smith's moral framework for *Wealth of Nations*, see Rebecca Todd Peters, "Economic Justice Requires More than the Kindness of Strangers," in *Global Neighbors: Christian Faith and Moral Obligation in Today's Economy*, ed. Douglas A. Hicks and Mark Valeri (Grand Rapids: Eerdmans, 2008), 89–108.

15. Information regarding the Kader fire is from William Greider's report of the incident found in William Greider, *One World, Ready or Not: The Manic Logic of Global Capitalism* (New York: Simon and Schuster, 1997), 339–346.

16. Joseph Berger, "100 Years Later, the Roll of the Dead in a Factory Fire Is Complete," *New York Times*, February 20, 2011, A13.

17. The 1908 Social Creed of the Churches that was adopted with the formation of the Federal Council of Churches was a public statement of the goals of the social gospel movement that focused on establishing a 40-hour workweek, abolishing child labor, and establishing a minimum wage, among other things.

18. Martin Luther King Jr., "Address at the Fourth Annual Institute on Nonviolence and Social Change at Bethel Baptist Church, December 3, 1959," in *The Papers of Martin Luther King, Jr, Volume 5: Threshold of a New Decade, January 1959–December 1960*, ed. Clayborne Carson (Los Angeles: University of California Press, 2005), 333–343.

19. Broadly speaking, critical social theory is a branch of intellectual inquiry that draws on a variety of disciplines, including history, social science, and philosophy, with the intention of critiquing and transforming society. See Max Horkheimer, "Traditional and Critical Theory," in *Critical Theory: Selected Essays*, trans. Matthew J. O'Connell (New York: Continuum, 2002).

20. Kwame Anthony Appiah, *Cosmopolitanism: Ethics in a World of Strangers* (New York: W.W. Norton, 2006).

21. For several decades, the task of liberation theology has been to encourage people living in situations of oppression and injustice place their own experience within a larger structural analysis that enables them to see the origins of the problem and help them envision concrete solutions that empower them to create social change. Since Paulo Freire's groundbreaking work in *Pedagogy of the Oppressed*, justice educators have focused on experiential education, or teaching people by involving them in the work and practice of social change. Paulo Freire, *Pedagogy of the Oppressed*, trans. Myra Bergman Ramos (New York: Continuum, 2000).

22. Robert Wuthnow, "Beyond Quiet Influence? Possibilities for the Protestant Mainline," in *Quiet Hand of God: Faith-Based Activism and the Public Role of Mainline Protestantism*, ed. Robert Wuthnow and John H. Evans (Berkeley: University of California Press, 2002), 389.

23. Beverly Wildung Harrison, "Theological Reflection in the Struggle for Liberation," in *Making the Connections*, ed. Carol Robb (Boston: Beacon, 1985), 245.

1

Theories of Solidarity

The term *solidarity* has been used in social, political, and religious discourse for over 200 years. However, very little attention has been given to defining and theorizing exactly what is meant by it.[1] The idea of solidarity has had concrete influences in two arenas in contemporary social life—politics and religion. The concept of *fraternité*, or brotherhood, is a precursor to solidarity and shares some of its meaning. Let us begin our examination of solidarity by looking into the familial nature of the term *fraternité*.

IN THE BEGINNING: *FRATERNITÉ*

The political idea of fraternity, or brotherhood, was built upon the foundation of the family and the social bonds that united its members. Some of the earliest converts to Christianity were Greco-Roman households that were built on filial and familial ties. Early Christian communities invoked the language of family to describe their relationship with fellow believers and thought of themselves as a family of faith. In the fourth century, monastic communities of religious men began to set themselves apart from society and refer to one another as "brothers" in the faith. By the sixth century, communities of women religious developed parallel models of sisterhood.

The use of the idea of brotherhood within Christianity was theological as well as social. In his teachings, Jesus radically redefined family by claiming, "Whoever does the will of God is my brother and sister and mother" (Mark 3:35). That the language of brotherhood was definitional for understanding the relationships between early members of the Christian community is evidenced by the frequency with which Paul addresses the recipients of his letters as "brothers." This language is theologically consistent with the emphasis on God as "Father" that develops within the early Christian community. While the association of God with a father was present in the Hebrew Scriptures, the metaphor of God *as* Father becomes an important image for understanding God in the early church.[2] While Jesus was understood as God's son, it was not until the second century that the theological proposition that Jesus *was* God became prominent, and not until the Council of Nicea in 325 that the doctrine of the Trinity became orthodox Christian theology.

By the Middle Ages, the idea of a "brotherhood" based on bonds other than blood or faith began to extend to the secular world to describe the social identities and ties shared by men in a particular profession such as merchants, artisans, and their apprentices.[3] Norwegian philosopher Steinar Stjernø argues that during this time and through the Enlightenment, as society generally grew more secular, the term *fraternity* gradually lost its religious connotations.[4] While the term is widely associated with the French Revolution through the rallying cry of "*liberté, egalité, fraternité*," it did not appear in the 1789 French political document *Declaration of the Rights of Man and the Citizen,* nor the next nine constitutional documents. It was not until the Constitution of 1848 that it appeared as a formal political concept in the governance of France.[5]

Philosopher John Rawls, an eminent scholar on issues of justice, noted that "[i]n comparison with liberty and equality, the idea of fraternity has had a lesser place in democratic theory. It is thought to be less specifically a political concept, not in itself defining any of the democratic rights."[6] The way that the principles of liberty and equality have been developed in Western political philosophy, these concepts primarily refer to the liberty or equality of the individual in relation to society. As such, they conform to the emphasis on the rights and responsibilities of individual persons that classic liberalism seeks to promote as the foundation of political organization.

Fraternity, by contrast, is more closely associated with rights and responsibilities that correspond to our relationships with particular groups of people to whom we are related by blood, faith, or other social bond. The idea of brotherhood was used in the French Revolution to promote feelings of friendship and camaraderie in ways that downplayed the occupational differences and class distinctions among the revolutionaries.[7] However, in contemporary rhetoric, the concept of fraternity refers more to moral obligations that we owe to people we claim as our "brothers" (or "sisters") than to individual political rights. As a concept rooted in the moral obligations that arise from social relationships, it is a more complex political concept than equality or liberty and stands at odds with the liberal foundations of individualism that undergird contemporary Western democracies. While the concept of fraternity or brotherhood has both religious and secular origins, the use of this term has largely been eclipsed by the term solidarity, which shares very similar associations. The concept of solidarity has also been used in both political theory and Christian theology, and we will examine its usage in each setting.

DEVELOPMENT OF SOLIDARITY IN POLITICAL THEORY

In 1821, French philosopher Charles Fourier published *Theorie de l'Unite,* in which he offers a new model for social and political organization based on the formation of utopian communities that he called phalanxes. These phalanxes, which were modeled after the housing of military personnel, allowed 1,500 people to live and work together in common households. For this reason, his work is seen as a forerunner to socialism. However, Fourier did not imagine the elimination of private property or class differences, but rather the formation of a harmonious society that was rooted in a shared feeling of community or solidarity.

While the term *solidarity* was present in the Napoleonic Code in 1804[8] to refer to the collective responsibility of debt repayment and insurance,[9] Fourier's use of the term two decades later developed several aspects of the term that reflect the complexity of the idea to this day. In keeping with Fourier's vision for self-sufficient communities where people were able to live in harmony and fulfillment, he uses the term *solidarity* in four distinct ways. First, like its legal usage in the Napoleonic Code, solidarity described a kind of social insurance that provided for a collective repayment of debt. Second, solidarity referred to a willingness to share resources with those in need. Third, it related to a general sentiment or feeling that a community of people held for one another. Finally, Fourier used it to indicate concrete public policies that would provide a guaranteed minimum to support families.[10] These four usages of solidarity—legal obligations, moral responsibility, sentiment, and public policy—reflect the disparate nature of the understanding of solidarity over the last two hundred years and help to explain why it has been difficult to build much consensus around the coherent use of the term.

Pierre Leroux, the next philosopher to use the term, understood the idea of solidarity as primarily about social relationships between people. In fact, he saw society as largely a social rather than a political entity, and he believed the purpose of socialism was to organize greater and greater solidarity in society. While Fourier's concept of solidarity had been limited to his utopian communities, Leroux understood the term as more broadly applicable to the organization of society as a whole. [11]

It is no coincidence that the idea of solidarity came to the fore in the early days of the Enlightenment and the Industrial Revolution as the focus in philosophy and political and legal theory began to shift from the community to the individual. As we saw with the term *fraternité*, solidarity is also an idea that stands in tension with the individualism that undergirds ideas of liberty and freedom. However, unlike *fraternité*, which is almost exclusively concerned with the communal aspects of relationship, solidarity is a concept that attempts to balance the individual and the community and to live into the tension between an increasing focus on individual rights and liberty and traditional concerns for the common or collective good. One of the most influential new ideas that dominated thinking in the eighteenth century, championed by Adam Smith, was the idea that the behavior of individuals pursuing their own self-interest in the market sphere would, in the aggregate, create a healthy and well-functioning society. There was a philosophical shift in which the social unit of attention moved from society as a whole to what is good for individual members of society.

Auguste Comte, a French philosopher who was one of the founders of the field of sociology, was opposed to the increasing individualism that accompanied the industrialization of production and the accompanying laissez-faire economic thinking.[12] As a budding sociologist, Comte was interested in examining and understanding the functioning of societies or groups of people. He recognized the tensions that existed between individualism and social well-being, but he emphasized that there is a radical interdependence that lies at the core of human life. This radical interdependence demonstrates the paradox of the worldview of individualism that was developing in his time. Even as industrialization and the development of assembly lines and manufacturing processes divided people and reduced them to cogs in a machine, people's radical dependence on one another was manifest by the fact that they must work together to produce the material goods needed to survive. Comte believed that because the processes of industrialization moved people toward separation and disunity, government must act deliberately to facilitate the development of a feeling of solidarity among its citizens.[13] Comte's rather vague use of solidarity to refer to a "feeling" that he assumed his readers would understand was developed in more detail in the work of Émile Durkheim.

Durkheim was the first person to systematically differentiate between different types of solidarity.[14] As a sociologist, Durkheim was interested in understanding what holds societies together. He was not swayed by the arguments of the social contract, self-interest, or rational calculation; he argued instead that society is held together by people's shared social bonds and values. Durkheim recognized that shifts in modern society were changing the ways in which these social bonds were shaped, formed, and adopted, but he held them to be essential to social cohesion nonetheless. He used the term *mechanical solidarity* to describe the bonds that hold people together in traditional society. These bonds reflect the similarities that people share in their life experience and worldview as these are shaped by common living conditions, culture, belief systems, religion and rituals.[15] Durkheim argued that traditional societies have strong bonds of solidarity that unite them because people in those societies share a common worldview and perspective on life. In modern societies—where there is more variation in life experience, culture, religious beliefs, education, and work experience—people do not share the same social bonds of tradition and values that characterize traditional societies. Here Durkheim picks up on Comte's characterization of the interdependence that characterizes human life, even in industrial societies.

Paradoxically, even as modern societies move toward a celebration of the individual, our actual lives are more dependent on one another as we move into specialized labor that requires us to rely even more on others to help us meet our daily needs. As society moved away from an agrarian and artisanal orientation—in which many people were able to provide for a large number of their day-to-day needs—to a more specialized and labor-saving model of economic production, our interdependence increased. As the work of each individual becomes more and more narrowly defined in an industrial society (and here Durkheim is referring exclusively to wage labor in the workforce), our capacity to meet a greater portion of our own needs declines. Thus, like the organs in the body that perform specialized functions but depend upon the healthy functioning of the whole in order to survive, the solidarity that is present in modern (industrial) societies is an *organic solidarity*. Because Durkheim held that solidarity was the social glue that held societies together, he was concerned that societies were shifting from a mechanical experience of solidarity to an organic experience of solidarity as modernity transformed the nature of work and our social relations in the process. He believed that stark differences in social inequities could interfere with the development of organic solidarity; thus all people should have access to pursue positions and experiences that corresponded to their natural abilities.[16] Social justice and equality were thus foundational to Durkheim's understanding of a healthy society bound together by the social bonds of organic solidarity.

While solidarity was not nearly as important a concept to Max Weber as it was to Durkheim, Weber used the idea of solidarity in two important ways that will bear on further discussions. First, Weber proposed that there are two distinct kinds of social relationships that govern how people behave in society. The first, which he refers to as *Vergemeinschaftung*, describes actions and behaviors that are exercised within the boundaries or confines of particular meaningful relationships. These actions are based on a shared sense of community and can be designated as reflecting a sense of social solidarity. The second kind of social relationship, *Vergesellschaftung*, is far removed from personal relationships and the corresponding social obligations and refers to actions that are taken exclusively for personal or material advantage.[17]

While there is not always a clear dividing line between these two types of relationships and behaviors, they do reflect two distinct ways of thinking about social, political, and economic actions in contemporary life. The first is governed through the social control of the community as decisions are made in the context of community and subject to the approbation or praise of one's colleagues, peers, family, and friends. The second is more appropriately governed by external controls that correspond to democratic principles of fairness and equality. Simply put, in relationships of solidarity there is an internal system of accountability, while relationships of exchange oriented toward material gain are governed by external authorities.

The second contribution that Weber makes to thinking about solidarity is that his description of groups or communities that exhibit solidarity demonstrates the importance of a shared feeling that binds them together in a way that offers a common identity—a "we," so to speak. For Weber, this necessarily presupposes an in-group and an out-group. If there is a "we," then there must also be a "they."[18] For the first time, the idea of solidarity is not just used to identify what binds groups of people together, but also to illustrate how this common bond may differentiate the group from others in potentially conflicting ways.

Stjernø points out that the development of the concept of solidarity within the political and social conditions of France in the early nineteenth century meant that it was originally employed by philosophers and thinkers interested in promoting stability and social order in the wake of the political unrest of the French Revolution and the Napoleonic empire.[19] Additionally, the development of capitalism and the social changes prompted by the Industrial Revolution also figured prominently in the development of solidarity as a sociological concept to help make sense of the changing social environment. As the term was taken over by German thinkers in the work of Max Weber and subsequently by Karl Marx and his followers, it took a decidedly political turn as it became more closely associated with the actions and identities of workers and worker movements. Weber's notion of confrontation and conflict came to play a more central role in the development of the concept of solidarity as it took root in the Marxist and socialist traditions.

While Marx did not use the term *solidarity* very frequently in his own writing, Stjernø argues that his work reflects two different ideas that correspond to the idea of solidarity.[20] The first kind of solidarity represents the relationships and bonds between members of the working class due to their common struggle against oppression under capitalism. It is this notion of working-class solidarity that will develop into the dominant form of political solidarity within the socialist party in the late nineteenth and twentieth centuries.

The second form of solidarity Stjernø identifies is an ideal or utopian version of solidarity that Marx envisions can only exist within communist societies. For Marx, it is only within the perfect freedom of communism that genuine and true social solidarity can be achieved among people. The first form of solidarity is an instrumental means of moving toward the true freedom and community that is only possible in a communist society.

It was one of Marx's followers, Karl Kautsky, who transformed the abstract rhetoric of feelings, social bonds, and relationships into concrete political action. Kautsky argued that "the goal of social democracy was to transform society into one where the economy was based upon solidarity."[21] By this he meant that worker ownership of the means of production and an emphasis on social or cooperative production offered a more stable and egalitarian economic foundation for society than the capitalist system, which produced great wealth for a small class of people and exploited the workers in the process.[22] Kautsky also argued that the political base of a social democratic party should move beyond the working class to include other working people who were exploited by capitalism and shared common concerns with the proletariat, who were traditionally defined as laborers who depended upon wage labor for survival in a capitalist system.

Despite attention to the concept of solidarity by these and other intellectuals in the eighteenth, nineteenth, and twentieth centuries, the concept of solidarity remains vague and insufficiently theorized to the extent that it is a word and a concept that means many things to many people. Its popular association with worker's movements through the popular song "Solidarity Forever" and the Polish labor movement's adoption of the name "Solidarity" in the 1980s has prompted many people to associate the term with communism and socialism. However, the term has been used far more broadly in political philosophy and has a rich history within the Christian tradition as well. The idea of solidarity offers fruitful possibilities for helping to think about faith commitments, political responsibilities, and relationships with neighbors—near and far.

DEVELOPMENT OF SOLIDARITY IN THEOLOGICAL DISCIPLINES

To the extent that the concept of solidarity reflects a deep relationship of affection and mutuality between individuals or groups of people, it is reminiscent of the guiding normative value of love that has shaped Christian theology and practice from the earliest days. In both its *agapē* (selfless love) and *philia* (love of friends and family) forms, love is a dominant theme in the New Testament and the early Christian church. The idea of solidarity in the social and political sense in which it is used by philosophers, social scientists, and politicians began to emerge in Christian thought in the late nineteenth century as both the Protestant and Catholic churches struggled alongside their secular counterparts to discern appropriate responses to the changing social and political world brought about by the Industrial Revolution.

Within Protestant churches in the late nineteenth and early twentieth centuries, the Social Gospel Movement in the United States and the Christian Socialist movement in Europe echoed the concerns raised by Auguste Comte, Émile Durkheim, and Max Weber about the growing tensions between an increasing individualism in capitalist society and the reality of human interdependence even in the modern world. The exploitation and suffering of workers and people living in poverty prompted Protestant ministers, leaders, and laypeople to develop a theology of justice and compassion that supported the needs and interests of exploited workers by working toward public policy reforms like minimum wages, worker safety, reasonable workweeks, and the elimination of child labor. In 1908, the Federal Council of Churches endorsed the "Social Creed of the Churches," which detailed an explicit public social agenda for Protestants that grew out of their faith commitments to justice and equality. While none of the Social Gospelers used the idea of solidarity as a major foundation for the development of their theology or their movement, their work in partnership with marginalized and oppressed workers to improve their social situation and to work toward justice in society reflects the heart of the idea of solidarity. The Social Gospel Movement relates to a longer tradition of social Christianity that reflects over a hundred-year commitment to the practice of solidarity as a concrete way to live out God's prophetic call to justice in our world.[23]

The shift from the Middle Ages to the world of the Enlightenment also caused the Roman Catholic Church to rethink its role and position in society, particularly in the political realm. While papal authority and the magisterium had a long history of collusion in political power and governance in Europe, the emerging democracies of the nineteenth century required Roman Catholics to rethink the relationship between politics and religion. In 1891, with the publication of *Rerum Novarum*, Pope Leo XIII signaled a new approach to the modern world that put the ancient alliances between throne and altar to rest.[24] *Rerum Novarum* established the papacy's commitment to a just social order by declaring allegiance to the poor and needy in society and by reminding Roman Catholics of their Christian obligation to charity. However, Leo XIII did not leave the responsibility of the poor solely to charity; he also called for social reforms that would redress the growing inequalities in society. Much like the Social Gospelers, without using the term *solidarity* the Roman Catholics called for Christians to develop ministries and actions of social justice that would lead to the development of social solidarity in society. The publication of *Rerum Novarum* is regarded as the beginning of what has come to be known as "Catholic social teaching," which is "the application of the word of God to people's lives and the life of society."[25]

Roman Catholic commitment to charity and social justice continued throughout the twentieth century. Pope John XXIII introduced the term *solidarity* into papal discourse in 1961 in *Mater et Magistra,* which was issued on the seventieth anniversary of *Rerum Novarum.* It was intended to update the Catholic Church's teaching on issues of poverty and the human condition in light of the many social and technological changes that had occurred in the intervening years. John XXIII described himself as taking up the torch of his predecessors in attempting to seek "appropriate solutions to the many social problems of our times"[26] when he called for government assistance for people in need and for government action to reduce economic inequality in societies and in the world at large.[27] His use of the term *solidarity* largely refers to the character of Christian relationships of "brotherhood," reinforcing some of the overlap between the ideas of solidarity and brotherhood, or *fraternité,* discussed earlier.[28] In 1967, Pope Paul VI issued *Populorum Progressio,* a papal encyclical that addressed "the development of peoples." Paul VI uses the term *solidarity* ten times in this statement, though his use largely describes solidarity as the characteristic that he thinks should define the attitudes and relationships that ought to exist between political entities or nation-states.[29]

Stjernø argues that the Roman Catholic concept of solidarity is rooted both in compassion and collective action to help the poor and underprivileged and in a recognition of the need to move beyond individual charity to address the depth and breadth of the problems of inequality that threaten our world. Solidarity finally becomes a prominent theme of Roman Catholic social teaching with the contributions of Pope John Paul II, who develops a much more vigorous usage of the term.[30] John Paul II carefully links the idea of solidarity with other key principles of Catholic social thought, including the common good, love, justice, and subsidiarity. *Sollicitudo Rei Socialis,* a papal encyclical issued in 1987, best represents his use of the idea of solidarity as an organizing principle for addressing social problems.

In *Sollicitudo,* John Paul II strongly critiques the reigning political discourse focused on the "logic of blocs" that characterized Cold War political divisions.[31] He denounces both "liberal capitalism" and "Marxist collectivism" as inadequate to respond to the pressing moral concerns of the day,[32] which he identifies as the problems of poverty, inequality, and underdevelopment. The theme of solidarity is such a prominent aspect of his charge for how the world should shape political and social relationships in ways that can effectively respond to these problems that Robert Ellsberg has characterized his proposed alternative as "the logic of solidarity."[33] For John Paul II, this logic of solidarity represents an interdependence between peoples and nations that reflects a commitment to the common good[34] and a theological affirmation that the "goods of creation are meant for all."[35] Yet because he is aware that ideas like solidarity, interdependence, and the common good are critiqued as being too closely associated with or influenced by Marxist collectivism, he also is careful to argue that solidarity must be balanced by freedom.[36] His interest in breaking the dichotomy of East/West and capitalism/communism prompts him to argue that attention to the common good that all humans share and the development of attitudes and relationships of solidarity offer a middle way through these tensions. For him, relationships of solidarity are rooted in the theological claim that people are to regard one another as moral equals who are "neighbors"; he also claims solidarity as a Christian virtue.[37] John Paul II focuses on solidarity as a concept that defines human relationships as bonds of family and friendship, which then form the basis for the development of societies that actually care for their citizens—especially those who are the most marginalized and in need of assistance.

However, the prominence of the term *solidarity* within Christian theological discourse is arguably due to the centrality of the concept in liberation theology. Gustavo Gutiérrez coined the term "liberation theology" in 1971 to describe a new theological movement that embodied the increasing commitment of priests, nuns, theologians, and churches to address the structural conditions of poverty in Latin America that contributed to the desperation of the majority of the poor.[38] Responding to the call of Pope John XXIII for the Second Vatican Council to recognize the Roman Catholic Church as the "church of the poor,"[39] religious leaders in Latin America began to conceive of a regional episcopal gathering that would take up this charge in light of the social context of poverty in which they lived and worked.

The Conference of Latin American Bishops in Medellín, Colombia in 1968 marked a new public stance of the Latin American church to renounce its privileges and to side with the poor and oppressed.[40] While this commitment to the poor and marginalized was in line with Catholic social teaching since *Rerum Novarum*, Medellín moved beyond calling Christians to respond to the situation of poverty in Latin America with a charitable heart. Rather, it sought to identify the structural foundations of poverty as a prelude to seeking social justice that would establish a meaningful peace in the region.[41] Prominent leaders like Gutiérrez, Oscar Romero, Leonardo Boff, and Jon Sobrino spoke out about the need for liberation from the oppression of poverty and repression that marked the sociopolitical context of many Latin American countries in the latter half of the twentieth century. In this struggle for liberation, solidarity was a principal theme.

Sobrino offered the most well-developed discussion of this theme in the 1982 book *Theology of Christian Solidarity*.[42] In it, he focused largely on the development of relationships of solidarity between churches from outside Latin America and Christians and churches in Latin America. Sobrino associated the desire of Christians to develop relationships of solidarity with the poor in Latin America during this time with their growing knowledge of the persecution of the church and its people.[43] Sobrino described these developing relationships of solidarity as the expression of the true mission of the Christian church—to live into the catholicity of the church as the one universal church that reflected and represented the oneness of God.[44]

The concept of solidarity within liberation theology began as an attitude that the institutional church ought to take as a way of supporting and helping to empower the poor. One of the principle tenets of liberation theology was the idea of the self-determination of the poor, which accompanied an increasing recognition that the liberation of the poor could not be left to the wealthy and elite. In response to *Populorum Progressio,* in which Paul VI proclaimed development as the new name for peace,[45] the "Message of the Bishops of the Third World" articulated a growing consensus that "the people of the poor and the poor of the peoples . . . know from experience that they must rely on themselves and their own strength, rather than on the help of the rich."[46] This emphasis on empowering the poor led to the development of base Christian communities (BCC) where marginalized people gathered together to study Scripture and to talk about how to create social change in their communities and their countries. Rather then seeing themselves as the leaders and instigators of this growing liberation movement, Latin American theologians argued that the institutional church needed to be in solidarity with the BCCs, meaning that the church would pledge to use its power, authority, and resources to support the liberation struggles of the people. In the Medellín statement, when the bishops called themselves to solidarity with the poor, they described this as making the problems and struggles of the poor their own.[47] Base Christian communities and liberation theology continued to grow throughout the 1970s, as did poverty and political repression in many parts of Latin America.

The idea of churches and individuals acting in solidarity with the churches and peoples of Latin America really took hold in the early 1980s in response to the political turmoil in Central America. This turmoil became increasingly more public with the murder of Archbishop Oscar Romero and four US Catholic women in 1980, the "disappearance" of countless civilians who were murdered by off-duty military personnel known as "death squads," and the influx of refugees into the United States seeking political asylum and sharing stories of the atrocities of civil war and paramilitary activity. As awareness of the political repression in various countries in Latin America grew, many US churches responded by organizing the "Sanctuary Movement." Sanctuary churches were local congregations that provided asylum and support for political refugees that the US government refused to recognize. In addition to addressing the needs of refugees, many of these people and their institutions understood their commitment to solidarity with Latin America to entail developing personal or ecclesial relationships with people and churches in Latin America, to travel to trouble spots as a way of raising attention to the issues, to lobby Congress to change US asylum laws, and to advocate for the closing of the "School of the Americas," a US government training facility in Georgia where many Latin American military leaders were trained in techniques of torture and repression. In this way, US churches and US Christians (and others) acted exactly the way Latin American theologians had called for the non-poor to respond. They reacted with solidarity with the poor and repressed in their region by using their status, power, influence, and financial resources to stand with the poor and marginalized as partners fighting together against injustice.[48]

In the years since the word *solidarity* began to be used in Latin American liberation theology, it has become ubiquitous as a clarion call in situations of injustice. It has been embraced by liberation and feminist theologians such as Beverly Harrison, Sharon Welch, Ada-Maria Isasi-Diaz, Mary Hobgood, and Anselm Min.[49] With the exception of Min, these feminist and liberation theologians have used the term *solidarity* to refer to relationships between people of privilege and people who are oppressed. While their projects have not been to offer a systematic definition of what they mean by solidarity, each author has emphasized aspects of solidarity that contribute to the development of a robust ethic of solidarity. Harrison highlights that solidarity requires accountability to oppressed people, Welch describes solidarity as the theoretical content of liberation theology, and Isasi-Diaz defines solidarity as the enactment of the gospel demand to love our neighbor.[50] Hobgood draws on feminist and liberationist definitions of solidarity as accountability and mutuality to dissect real experiences where solidarity was lacking in an effort to examine what accountability to "world-majority" women would look like.[51] Min, whose work is the most recent, identifies himself as a liberation theologian but develops a theology of "solidarity of others" as a new paradigm that he argues moves beyond liberation theology.[52] For Min, liberation theology has been too focused on the differences that separate people. The idea of "solidarity of others" that he offers is meant to be a new way of seeing human relationships as based on interdependence rather than individualism (which he sees as promoting the idea of difference).

SOLIDARITY AS THE FOUNDATION FOR SOCIAL CHANGE

Historically, solidarity has been a challenging and rigorous principle. It continues to hold the potential to offer people of privilege a transformative avenue for engaging the world and using their privilege for the common good. However, the casual usage of the term to describe everything from purchasing a handbag,[53] to donating money, signing a petition, or wearing a bracelet risks undermining solidarity's potential for the kind of social change prompted by something like the Sanctuary Movement. Furthermore, the danger of connecting the practice of solidarity with the consumptive activity of shopping is that it threatens to undermine the power of the term to encourage people to engage in a structural critique of the patterns of global capitalism that are contributing to the continued impoverishment of many of the poorest of the poor. While it would be foolhardy to try to rescue solidarity from the many ways in which its usage belittles its deeper transformational aspects, it is useful to think carefully about the ways in which the idea of solidarity can serve as the foundation for a transformation ethic for people of privilege.

Within theological discourse, the principle of solidarity has primarily developed in three concrete ways. The first way focuses on how base Christian communities (or other communities of poor and near-poor people) work together with one another as support networks for engaging in the process of social change. The second way focuses on how the institutional church (or churches) can develop ecclesial relationships of solidarity with the poor in order to take up their cause, to partner with them in development, resistance, and justice, and to speak for them when they lack access or voice. The third way is as a strategy or tool that can contribute to the support of a short-term action, campaign, or relief effort.

Both of the first two usages of solidarity indicate a longer-term commitment to partnership and long-term social change, while the third usage is an attempt to capitalize on the moral value of the first two usages in order to leverage short-term support for a particular agenda. Because the concept of solidarity has been so closely tied to liberation theology for the past forty years, each of these approaches begins with the reality of the poor and marginalized as its starting point. What has yet to be fully developed is an ethic of solidarity that starts from the reality of life in the first world and that focuses on the ways in which solidarity can offer people of privilege opportunities to build relationships and networks of solidarity that allow them to build new lives rooted in the interdependence of the human community reflected in the mandate to love your neighbor as yourself. Because a first-world ethic of solidarity begins from a position of privilege rather than a position of marginalization, analyzing and understanding privilege must be its starting point.

Notes

1. Two scholars have paid significant attention to examining the history and meaning of this concept. German philosopher Kurt Bayertz organized a conference on the topic in 1994 with two colleagues and subsequently edited a book, *Solidarity*, ed. Kurt Bayertz (Dordrecht, The Netherlands: Kluwer Academic, 1999). The book's twenty contributors examine both the history of this idea and how it has been used and appropriated in different disciplines and spheres of society. In 2004, Steinar Stjernø published a more in-depth intellectual history of solidarity, *Solidarity in Europe: The History of an Idea* (Cambridge: Cambridge University Press, 2004). This book traces the history of the concept through its two primary manifestations in European tradition, social theory and theology. Additionally, in 2008, philosopher Sally J. Scholz examined how the concept of solidarity might contribute to a theory of political solidarity, *Political Solidarity* (University Park, PA: Penn State, 2008).

2. See Sallie McFague, *Metaphorical Theology: Models of God in Religious Language* (Minneapolis: Fortress, 1982), and *Models of God: Theology for an Ecological, Nuclear Age* (Philadelphia, Fortress, 1987) for detailed discussion about the use and value of metaphorical language for the divine.

3. Stjernø, *Solidarity in Europe,* 26–27.

4. Ibid., 27.

5. Véronique Munoz-Dardé, "Fraternity and Justice," in *Solidarity,* ed. Kurt Bayertz (Dordrecht, The Netherlands: Kluwer Academic, 1999), 94, n.3.

6. John Rawls, *A Theory of Justice* (Cambridge: Harvard University Press, 1971), 105.

7. Stjernø, *Solidarity in Europe,* 27.

8. Sven-Eric Liedman, "Solidarity," trans. Ken Schubert, *Eurozine*, 2002, originally published as *Att se sig själv i andra: Om solidaritet* (Bonnier Essä, 1999).

9. Stjernø, *Solidarity in Europe*, 28.

10. Ibid., 28.

11. Ibid., 29.

12. Ibid., 31.

13. Liedman, "Solidarity," 4.

14. Kurt Bayertz, "Four Uses of 'Solidarity,'" in *Solidarity*, ed. Kurt Bayertz (Dordrecht, The Netherlands: Kluwer Academic, 1999), 12. Durkheim develops his analysis of solidarity in Émile Durkheim, *The Division of Labor in Society* (1893, trans. W. D. Halls, 1933; repr., New York: Free Press, 1997).

15. Stjernø, *Solidarity in Europe*, 33.

16. Ibid., 34–35.

17. Ibid., 37.

18. Ibid., 38.

19. Ibid., 39.

20. Ibid., 46.

21. Ibid., 48.

22. Karl Kautsky, *The Class Struggle (Erfurt Program)*, 1892, trans. William E. Bohn (Chicago: Charles H. Kerr, 1910).

23. For more detail about the history and development of social Christianity, see Gary Dorrien, *Soul in Society: The Making and Renewal of Social Christianity* (Minneapolis: Fortress Press, 1995).

24. Stjernø, *Solidarity in Europe*, 64.

25. John Paul II, *Sollicitudo Rei Socialis*, encyclical letter on social concern, December 30, 1987, as quoted in Robert Ellsberg, *The Logic of Solidarity: Commentaries on Pope John II's Encyclical "On Social Concern,"* ed. Gregory Baum and Robert Ellsberg (Maryknoll, NY: Orbis, 1989), ix.

26. John XXIII, *Mater et Magistra*, encyclical letter on Christianity and social progress, May 15, 1961, 50.

27. Stjernø, *Solidarity in Europe*, 68.

28. In *Mater et Magistra* he uses the term *solidarity* three times in the sense of brotherhood/*fraternité* (23, 155, 157), and twice in a more generic sense of human connection and relationship (146, 190).

29. Paul VI, *Populorum Progressio,* encyclical letter on the development of peoples, March 26, 1967. These references are found in paragraphs 44, 48, 52, 62, 64, 65, 73, and 84. In addition to these eight references, he once uses the phrase "human solidarity" to describe an obligation associated with being part of the human species (17) and once as a Christian obligation associated with hospitality (67).

30. John Paul II's experiences of living in Poland through Nazi occupation, studying theology in both Poland and Rome, teaching and serving as bishop in Poland during the Soviet era, and serving as Pope during the rise of liberation theology in Latin America certainly all contributed in significant ways to his own understanding of the meaning and importance of the concept of solidarity. See Kevin P. Doran, *Solidarity: A Synthesis of Personalism and Communalism in the Thought of Karol Wojtyla/Pope John Paul II* (New York: Peter Lang, 1996) for an analysis of how John Paul II's understanding of solidarity is influenced by both communalism and personalism. See also Baum and Ellsberg, *The Logic of Solidarity*, for extended discussion of his use of solidarity in *Sollicitudo Rei Socialis.*

31. John Paul II, *Sollicitudo Rei Socialis*, 20.

32. Ibid., 21.

33. Baum and Ellsberg, *The Logic of Solidarity*, xi.

34. John Paul II, *Sollicitudo Rei Socialis*, 38.

35. Ibid., 39.

36. Ibid., 33.

37. Ibid., 39–40.

38. Gustavo Gutiérrez, *A Theology of Liberation: History, Politics and Salvation* (Maryknoll, NY: Orbis, 1973).

39. Gustavo Gutiérrez, "The Meaning and Scope of Medellin," in *The Density of the Present: Selected Writings* (Maryknoll, NY: Orbis, 1999), 67.

40. Ibid., 79.

41. Ibid., 87–88.

42. Jon Sobrino and Juan Hernandez Pico, *Theology of Christian Solidarity* (Maryknoll: Orbis, 1985; originally published 1982).

43. Ibid., 6–7.

44. Ibid., 12.

45. Paul VI, *Populorum Progressio*, 76.

46. Gutierrez, "Meaning and Scope," 77.

47. Latin American Bishops, "Poverty of the Church" (Conference of Latin American Bishops, Medellín, Colombia, September 6, 1968), para. 10.

48. In 1985, James McGinnis published *Solidarity with the People of Nicaragua*, outlining the ways in which US Christians could act in solidarity with the people of Nicaragua in an attempt to not only support them in their struggle but to work to change US policies that were covertly supporting the Contras in their attempt to destabilize the ruling Sandinista social democratic party that had overthrown the Somoza dictatorship. James McGinnis, *Solidarity with the People of Nicaragua* (Maryknoll, NY: Orbis, 1985).

49. Beverly Wildung Harrison, "Theological Reflection in the Struggle for Liberation," in *Making the Connections: Essays in Feminist Social Ethics*, ed. Carol Robb (Boston: Beacon, 1985), 235–66; Sharon Welch, *Communities of Resistance and Solidarity: A Feminist Theology of Liberation* (Maryknoll, NY: Orbis, 1985); Ada Maria Isasi-Diaz, "Solidarity: Love of Neighbor in the 1980s," in *Feminist Theological Ethics: A Reader*, ed. Lois K. Daly (Louisville: Westminster John Knox, 1994), 77–87; Mary Elizabeth Hobgood, "Solidarity and the Accountability of Academic Feminists and Church Activists to Typical (World-Majority) Women," *Journal of Feminist Studies in Religion* 20, no. 2 (2004): 137–65; Anselm Min, *The Solidarity of Others in a Divided World: A Postmodern Theology after Postmodernism* (New York: T&T Clark, 2004).

50. Harrison, "Theological Reflection," 244; Welch, *Communities of Resistance and Solidarity*, 46; Isasi-Diaz, "Solidarity" 78.

51. Hobgood, "Solidarity and Accountability," 137–49.

52. Min, *The Solidarity of Others*, 3.

53. "Scarlett Johansson Designs a Handbag for Haiti," *Oxfam International* press release, last modified February 4, 2010, http://www.oxfam.org/en/pressroom/pressrelease/2010-02-04/scarlett-johansson-designs-handbag-haiti.

2

Foundations for Transformation

As we can see by examining the intellectual history of the concept of solidarity, while it has been used consistently by a variety of theorists, theologians, activists, and political leaders, a certain lack of theoretical attention has led to a wide range of usages that trend from the general and ephemeral evocation of solidarity as a feeling or sentiment to something as concrete and specific as a labor movement in Poland. Journalist Christopher Hayes has situated solidarity on a continuum that ranges from "pearl-clutching pity through sympathy and empathy to arrive finally at solidarity, wherein you are propelled to do something for your fellow human-beings, to act as if their interests were your own."[1] He defines the ends of the spectrum as ranging from the mundane (a kind of feel-good, "one-for-all, all-for-one-ness") to the sublime (a "moral aspiration to realize the fundamental fellowship of humanity").[2]

However, not all of the actions that people take, even actions that are intended to "help," should be characterized as acts of solidarity. Hayes is accurate in identifying a continuum of emotions and behaviors as people respond to pressing issues of social justice in society. However, this continuum is not one of solidarity; rather, it is more accurate to think of it as a continuum of moral intuition. Moral intuition is a term that describes deeply felt reactions to moral situations that motivate people to action and moral reflection.[3] Morality refers to human understanding about what is right and wrong. While moral norms are shaped by human culture, there do seem to be certain moral standards that resonate across cultures and historical time periods. The moral norm of social justice is a guiding moral norm in the Christian tradition that is also cross-cultural and transhistorical. From a theological perspective, social justice demonstrates a desire to structure society in ways that recognize and honor the intrinsic value of creation and reflect God's concern for the well-being of all people and the created order.

Moral Habits

All humans are moral agents who make a variety of moral decisions every day, almost without thinking. Driving the speed limit, recycling, and refraining from littering are all moral actions. Most people are taught moral practices and behaviors by their parents, teachers, or other mentors. Sometimes, particular moral actions are a result of a specific moral dilemma that prompted a person to make a conscious decision about their moral behavior—maybe their speeding caused a wreck, or their friends shoplifted in junior high school and wanted them to join in—at such a point, they were confronted with the necessity of making a conscious decision about their moral behavior. Regardless of whether these moral actions are the result of conscious moral decisions or ingrained virtuous behavior, people engage in so many moral acts every day that actions like driving the speed limit, recycling, and refraining from littering become moral *habits* that people enact on a daily basis. This means that people do not necessarily think about each of these decisions as they make them; these actions have simply become part of one's daily routine. Nevertheless, these actions are moral actions in the sense that if people are asked to consciously think about them and argue whether it is right or wrong to speed, recycle, or litter, there is a readily identifiable consensus about the morally correct behavior in these circumstances.

It is possible to shape and change these moral habits. For people who know that their moral habits are lax—for instance, they have a tendency to lie or to speed—it is possible to develop more virtuous habits and to integrate these behaviors into a daily routine. There are other people who are simply not aware that their actions are morally dubious, if not downright harmful. For these people, sometimes correcting their behavior is simply an issue of education. For example, if someone is raised in a household where littering is common or they have never been exposed to recycling, it is necessary to educate them about the harmful results of their actions in order to prompt them to participate in the moral norms of a particular society or community. Actions that fall within the category of moral habits are generally those that are fairly straightforward and are commonly accepted across society. Of course, even within these fairly clear-cut moral norms, there are certainly instances when it may be morally acceptable to *break* these moral norms; for example, speeding when driving a woman in labor to the hospital.

MORAL INTUITIONS

In addition to the moral habits that are part of everyday life, people must constantly negotiate complex moral situations that are new or unfamiliar. When people encounter new moral questions or dilemmas they often respond automatically, out of gut moral intuitions that are shaped and formed by the intersections of their social location, worldview, and values. Moral intuition functions as a sort of moral compass that helps people assess what is right or wrong in a given situation. However, often when people think about their own moral agency or how they exercise their moral decision-making skills, they do not think about these everyday kinds of actions. Rather, the topics that are associated with moral decision-making are those that are fraught with moral ambiguity. Most thoughtful people recognize that the world in which we live is morally gray. This is often why people on the extreme ends of morally difficult questions like assisted suicide, abortion, and globalization tend to find their arguments falling on the deaf ears of the majority of US American citizens. Most people recognize that there is a moral complexity at the heart of these issues that warrants careful attention as they try to make morally difficult decisions about what is right and just. At the same time, most people receive very little training in how to exercise their moral agency. However, this does not mean that people are not morally reflective or that they do not have very real and strong visceral reactions to the moral problems that they encounter.

Social psychologist Jonathan Haidt has theorized that this intuitive response to moral judgments is a social intuitionist approach. This challenges the prevailing thought in social psychology that moral judgment involves a complex process of moral reasoning.[4] The rationalist school of social psychology argues that people go through "stages of moral development" that correspond to an increasingly sophisticated capacity to engage in moral reasoning.[5] From a rationalist perspective, people's moral judgments reflect a more or less developed capacity for moral reasoning. Haidt argues, rather, that people respond intuitively to moral conundrums and then search for moral reasons that support their intuitions.[6]

In recent years, the stories from Abu Ghraib and Guantanamo prompted thoughtful and productive public conversations about torture and due process within a normative understanding of what is acceptable behavior with regard to people who are suspected of being enemies of the state. Yet before people were even able to articulate clear, thoughtful, and rational arguments about why the behavior at Abu Ghraib and Guantanamo was immoral, many people who looked at the photos of prisoners being tortured responded out of their own moral intuition that such behavior was morally unacceptable.

When faced with new moral questions, people often respond automatically out of visceral moral intuitions that are shaped and formed by the intersection of their social location, their worldview, and their values. As people encounter and consider a wide variety of tragedies and social injustice that mark our world, their moral intuition and subsequent responses can be characterized in a variety of ways. These responses form a continuum of moral agency that ranges from sympathy to responsibility to mutuality. As we shall see in the next chapter, solidarity is a particular theological concept with specific requirements that not all of the categories of moral intuition reflect.

A closer examination of these categories of moral intuition allows us to see how they can be part of a pathway toward transformation that can lead to a place of solidarity. These categories of moral intuition exist along a continuum and are meant to offer the broadest strokes for helping people understand both the characteristics and behaviors of each category, while also illuminating the underlying theological implications of each position. They describe the ways in which contemporary first-world citizens respond to social and political crises as well as natural disasters around the world. Each category reflects distinct worldviews and theological perspectives about privilege, blessing, God, and what it means to be human. These categories describe the attitudes of people of privilege—whether earned or unearned—and how they think about and interact with people living on the margins of society. The complicity of persons whose actions and inactions support the status quo is a morally significant issue. From the perspective of social justice, the categories described here are not morally neutral. The fact that most people are not aware of the exact ways in which their actions are complicit in the exploitation of other people and the planet does not make their position morally neutral. The first two categories, sympathy and responsibility, represent where the majority of first-world Christians are currently positioned in relation to people living in poverty in all areas of the world. The third category, mutuality, offers the possibility of a new consciousness from which an ethic of solidarity can be built that might offer a countercultural paradigm for global relations and social structures.

Sympathy

The first category of moral intuition is sympathy. In this stage, people respond to the needs of others out of a feeling or emotion of sympathy or pity. They are moved by the pictures they see on television or newspaper reports about poverty, sweatshops, hunger, disease, climate change, and natural disaster. They react with moral indignation and horror to tragic events that sweep our consciousness. They are gripped by the crises of the moment, whether it is the

Asian tsunami, the tragedy in New Orleans following Hurricane Katrina, or the genocide in Darfur. They are compassionate people who care about others and feel a deep desire to reach out to them and help them in some way. People who act out of a moral intuition of sympathy often associate their own moral agency, or capacity to help or respond, with their privilege. This help often translates into writing a check, though it can extend to volunteering at a homeless shelter or participating in a mission trip to an impoverished country or work camp designed to clean up after a natural disaster. Primarily, people who respond from a moral intuition of sympathy are motivated either by feelings of pity and sorrow for the misfortunes of others, or by the guilt they feel when they judge that their lives are "better" than the lives of those they reach out to help. Individuals moved by sympathy might wear a wristband in "solidarity" with the One campaign to make poverty history, buy a Product Red shirt at the Gap to help fight AIDS in Africa, or write a check to a local charity. The emotional connection that they have for the plight of the victims/survivors of terrorism, HIV, poverty, or natural disaster is very real, and their desire to help is genuine.

Though it may not be explicitly stated, for people who act out of the sympathy stage of moral intuition, there is a fundamental divide that exists between them and the "other" they seek to help. While their sympathies are roused by the immediacy of the news story or as long as they are looking at the footage of the tragedy in question, the distance that separates them from these "others" allows them to turn the channel, put down the newspaper, or simply turn away and continue to lead their lives the same way that they did before they learned of this latest catastrophe. In *The Theory of Moral Sentiments*, Adam Smith describes this kind of behavior when he imagines the reactions of a European man to a disastrous earthquake in China. Smith acknowledges that a "man of humanity in Europe" would certainly respond with sympathy to the plight of the victims of the earthquake, and might even reflect on the precariousness of life itself. After further considering the effects that this disaster might have on global commerce, Smith suggests that this man would most likely return to the normal business of his day without a further thought for the millions of people affected by the earthquake in China.[7] Despite a distance of over two hundred years, Smith's description of sympathetic behavior is an accurate description of how many first-world people in our day deal with poverty and disaster in the developing world.

People who act out of sympathy lack an understanding of, or simply avoid thinking about, the systemic factors that have contributed to the social injustice or tragedy that has moved them to act. For the most part, their personal experience of privilege is an assumed part of their life and remains relatively unexamined. Many Christians who act out of this category of moral intuition also share a theological understanding of their privilege, success, or (relative) affluence as a blessing from God. They thank God for their health, their good jobs, their families, and for the blessing of living in a country where they have the freedom to succeed and thrive. These prayers reveal belief in a potentially dangerous theology of blessing that allows people to understand their privilege as gifts from God. While the origins of this kind of theology can be traced to Calvinist and Puritan ideals about humility and the beneficence of God, in an increasingly integrated world that is marked by unconscionable disparities of wealth and poverty, this kind of theology implies that the poor people in our world, including whole countries of people, have *not* been blessed by God. The deeper theological implication is that the people who live in the first world are somehow morally superior to those who live in the two-thirds world. This kind of theology ignores the very real material circumstances of human sin that have created economic injustice through colonialism, imperialism, human trafficking, and greed. While the desire of people to not seem as if they "deserve" the many material goods that make up their life might be laudable, a theology that serves to justify their wealth as a gift or blessing from God creates divine sanctification for the social inequality in our world. This, in turn, can function to reinforce an uninformed worldview that explains world poverty through the lens of individual responsibility that is foundational to neoliberalism.

RESPONSIBILITY

Responsibility is the second category of moral intuition. In this stage, people recognize that society is plagued by social problems and that they hold a certain amount of privilege. Their recognition of these two facts motivates them to act to help others out of an understanding that their privilege and relative affluence gives them a certain authority and accountability to care for others who are less fortunate. While they may have some awareness of the historic injustices in our country as they relate to race and gender, many people in this stage are still guided by a deep faith in the principles of liberty and freedom, and champion individual rights and equality of opportunity as the solution to inequality. Often, they believe that democratic societies have progressed to a place where all people really do have the capacity to change their situation in life if they just work hard enough and make good life choices. This might lead them to work with organizations that focus on providing relief and support to individuals who have experienced misfortune or personal crisis. Sometimes, belief in the possibilities that liberty and freedom offer can mask their ability to see the structural aspects of race, class, gender and other oppressions that function to interfere with people's attempts to help themselves or better their situations.

Many people in this stage have developed or are in the process of developing a more critical assessment of globalization. In light of the problems of sweatshops, forced labor, human trafficking, and environmental degradation that they associate with recent trends in globalization, they do not necessarily buy into the dominant rhetoric that free trade is the solution to poverty in the developing world. They are often aware of their own complicity in perpetuating these same problems, but are at a loss in imagining how they can make a difference in the world. Increasingly, one way in which they are responding is to try to be more accountable with their own purchasing power and to seek out personal lifestyle changes that they can implement—like installing low-energy light bulbs; buying local, organic, and/or fair trade food; or boycotting Walmart and other big box retailers that have reputations for the exploitation of workers domestically and internationally. These kinds of direct actions have the benefit that a certain amount of personal control over one's buying power can offer immediate gratification and a feeling of satisfaction in an often-overwhelming global economy. Yet while many people who act out of a moral intuition of responsibility recognize that their individual actions can never possibly make a dent in the problem, most of them have not yet grasped the kind of large-scale attitudinal shift required by the project of long-term social change.

People who work out of a moral intuition of responsibility are part of a deep tradition of privileged people acting benevolently to help those less fortunate than themselves. The danger of acting out of this intuition is that it betrays an imbalance of power in the relationship between the two parties, implying that one is responsible and therefore morally good while the person in need is in some way irresponsible and therefore morally flawed. The group needing assistance is represented as helpless and lacking agency. It was this same kind of flawed theological anthropology, positioning one group of people as morally or intellectually superior to another, that was the foundation of white supremacy, or the belief that the white "race" is morally and intellectually superior to other "races." When inequality is embedded in our theological anthropology, it functions to keep a certain distance between the two parties. This kind of relationship is often referred to as paternalism, in that the economic or social inequality between the two parties sets up a situation of perceived moral or social superiority that hampers genuine social and political solidarity.

Like the people in the previous category, most people who act out of a moral intuition of responsibility do so with the best of intentions and a desire to help. However, our actions may actually contribute to increased inequality and exploitation when we approach "the other" from a position of responsible paternalism or benevolence. As long as first-world people think of themselves as "responsible" for addressing the problems of poverty, they position themselves as experts in ways that disempower the voice, perspective, and agency of people living in poverty.

A more positive way to think about the responsibility of the first world to the two-thirds world with regard to issues of poverty and justice would be to think in terms of reparation or restitution for the damage that slavery and colonialism have done to the economic and social development of the two-thirds world. This approach, however, would require that people in the first world relinquish their paternalistic attitude to foreign aid so that reparation funds would not simply be used to further a first-world agenda of increased economic integration and capitalist production. Rather, the expenditure of funds of this sort could be mutually negotiated through democratic processes that facilitated the participation of broad sectors of civil society. This would allow for the meaningful participation of people living in poverty who have alternative visions for what sort of economic development would further the well-being of their communities, rather than primarily focusing on increasing a nation's GDP.

From a theological perspective, the inequalities of power, education, resources, and political influence that exist between the wealthy and the poor (be they individuals or nations), defy God's intention for the creation of a world where social justice marks the common life of God's created order. God did not endorse an ethic of paternalism by telling people to love their neighbors as they love their children; rather, the commandment to "love your neighbor as yourself" is a commandment of equality, which forms the foundation of an ethic of solidarity. Furthermore, if people considered how they would like to be treated if the situations of the global North and South were reversed, the importance of relationship, partnership, and the democratic participation of people affected by the problems that need to be remediated might become more apparent.

MUTUALITY

Mutuality is the final category of moral intuition. From a position of mutuality, people act to help others out of an understanding that the well-being of all creation is interdependent. In a relationship of mutuality, there is a desire to know one another and to develop a relationship of partnership and respect that contributes to the ongoing well-being of both parties. This category of moral intuition offers the possibility of a new way of responding to injustice that focuses on building relationships between people whose lives are marked by social and economic difference and working together to address the problem. A foundation of respect for other people's worldviews and life experiences allows people from different backgrounds and social locations to engage one another in a dialogue that can help lead to the development of new solutions to age-old problems. Too often, when people work out of a position of sympathy or responsibility, they think they know how to solve problems on behalf of others. People who work out of a position of mutuality understand that they can work together with others to solve social problems that impact everyone, but they cannot solve other people's problems for them. Partnerships based on mutuality demonstrate a capacity for multiple parties to use their strengths and assets to work together toward the common good.

A position of mutuality is rooted in a theological anthropology that affirms the goodness of all God's creation and recognizes that all human beings were created in God's image. People who work out of a moral intuition of mutuality reflect a worldview that differs from the dominant focus on individuality and difference and allows people to meet one another as moral equals. Of course, it is difficult to establish relationships of mutuality when discrepancies of income, wealth, education, and other forms of social privilege remain between parties. In these situations, "moral equality" is a philosophical or theological position that can become the basis for building a social relationship of solidarity. As such, mutuality is a different foundational starting point than either sympathy or responsibility. Those who act out of a moral intuition of mutuality recognize the capricious nature of human existence, whereby one's country of origin and the class status of one's parents have a far stronger correlation to one's own future than innate intellect or ability. The motivation that comes from a moral intuition of mutuality is cognizant of the social factors of politics, power, wealth, and greed that contribute to the creation of social structures that disproportionately benefit the educated and wealthy classes.

Sometimes, what is needed to address a particular crisis is simply money. In these instances, sympathetic responses of charitable giving are a faithful first step in responding to one's neighbor. But for those people who recognize the interdependence of the web of life, possessing (or cultivating) a moral intuition of mutuality challenges one to think beyond the immediate needs to ask deeper questions about the causes of a problem. For these people, seeking relationships of mutuality with those people who are most deeply affected by these problems can prompt more strategic reflection about effective and justice-oriented responses to the injustice in our midst. Certainly, it is not possible for people who are motivated by an affirmation of the mutuality of life to seek to develop relationships of solidarity with all those who are the victims of global injustice. However, an orientation of mutuality is a necessary moral foundation for first-world people who desire to develop such relationships as part of a journey to live more faithfully and more justly in the world.

SOLIDARITY AS THE FOUNDATION FOR SOCIAL CHANGE

Each of these categories of moral intuition helps to describe the way in which people respond on an instinctive level to problems of global injustice. These categories also correspond to Haidt's social intuitionist approach to moral judgment and affirm his assertion that moral intuition is somewhat akin to an aesthetic judgment that one might make when "one sees or hears about a social event and one instantly feels approval or disapproval."[8] But gut reactions and intuitions are not synonymous with ethical reflection and action. As a social psychologist, Haidt is interested in describing moral judgments; as an ethicist, I am interested in examining people's capacity for moral growth and development.[9] While I agree with Haidt that people often make instantaneous moral judgments that lack critical reflection and moral reasoning, for many people moral intuitions are merely a starting place. In describing the role that moral intuition should play in ethical reasoning, ethicist Beverly Harrison commented, "I believe we are right when we value feeling as the point of departure for our reasoning, but unwise when we endorse complete reliance on it as a full and sufficient theory."[10] Because moral intuitions represent visceral reactions rather than thoughtful reflection and analysis, they are also subject to manipulation by media outlets, politicians, or unscrupulous corporations seeking to exploit guilt and prejudices in order to further their own agendas. While some people may simply act out of their moral intuitions, a more morally responsible course of action is for people to employ their moral agency to engage in ethical reflection that can help people discern how God is calling them to respond in word and in deed to the injustice in the world. Moral agency is the term that is used to describe the human capacity to make judgments about what is right and wrong and to act accordingly. When people become more skilled moral agents by developing the tools of social analysis and theological reflection, it can improve moral responses to social injustice by focusing those responses on addressing structural problems that can lead to long-term social change.

The immediacy of natural and human-made disasters like tornadoes, hurricanes, earthquakes, tsunamis, and terrorism often generate immediate initial economic outpouring of sympathy from a broad spectrum of people. The Center on Philanthropy at Indiana University has documented elevated levels of philanthropic giving associated with September 11, the Indonesian tsunami, Hurricane Katrina, and the earthquake in Haiti. In the six months following each of these disasters, private donations from the United States spiked to generate between $1.4 billion (Haiti) and $3.9 billion (Katrina).[11] In 2005, there was a $15-billion increase in charitable giving with roughly half of this increase targeted to three events: the Indonesian tsunami, Hurricane Katrina, and the earthquake in Pakistan.[12] In each of these cases, hundreds of thousands of people followed the stories, horror-stricken by the conditions of death and human suffering. Many people responded in the way that Adam Smith described earlier by expressing compassion as they attempted to understand and make sense of these tragedies. Some people were moved to send money or donate blood or clothing or medical supplies to help the victims. Others got even more deeply involved by joining cleanup efforts, organizing mission trips, or getting their churches to sponsor refugee families.

There are a number of biblical stories that ground the dominant response of charity that permeates Christian culture and behavior. In Matt 25:31-46, Jesus lists caring for those who are hungry and thirsty, clothing the naked, welcoming the stranger, caring for the sick and visiting prisoners as the acts of righteous followers who, by engaging in these actions, have also demonstrated their love of the body of Christ as symbolized by the people of God. From the Good Samaritan to the message of John the Baptist that the people need to share their wealth with those who are needy, the Scriptures are full of admonitions to individuals to share their abundance with those who are in need.

But perhaps Christians only *think* that these passages represent the dominant view of how God calls us to respond to poverty because that is how we have been trained to think about responding to poverty. Charity is an essential aspect of both human and Christian responses to injustice. Witnessing the victims of natural disasters, disease epidemics, and malnutrition moves many people to engage in providing relief. Likewise, hearing people's stories of illness, house fires, or other calamities inspires many people to try to offer help. Providing the people who are right in front of us with immediate relief is the work of charity that wells out of the heart of human kindness.

The moral motivations of sympathy and responsibility that prompted people to respond to their neighbors in need are essential for human community and relationship. The ability to feel compassion and to feel responsible for one's actions, privileges, or fellow human beings are critical motivations that generate essential financial and material support for addressing the immediate needs of victims of natural and human-made disaster. In the aftermath of tragedy, the necessary immediate relief often requires a considerable amount of financial capital. The donations that result from the outpourings of sympathy and compassion of people unaffected by these tragedies are one embodiment of the commandment to "love your neighbor." These efforts are necessary and important acts of human kindness and *agapē* love that reach out to assist those in need.

But the reality is that these acts of human kindness, whether motivated by compassion or responsibility, like the actions of the good Samaritan, are ultimately acts of charity that address immediate needs without challenging the structural roots of injustice. Deeper ethical reflection about these issues requires rigorous social analysis around the social, political, and economic factors that contributed to the enormity of the devastation in each of these instances. It also requires the building of relationships of mutuality with those people who are most deeply affected by these problems in order to think more strategically together about effective and justice-oriented responses to the injustice in our midst. Likewise, first-world citizens and non-Gulf coast residents who considered themselves fairly removed from these events need to consider the contribution that disproportionate greenhouse emissions from first-world countries have made to the ongoing crisis of climate change. Long-term analysis of philanthropic giving indicates that these spikes in charitable donations are simply that: spikes that respond to the immediate tragedy but do not translate into long-term increases in giving or sustained attention to underlying structural problems.[13]

It is likely that the robbers on the road between Jerusalem and Jericho returned another day to rob another innocent traveler, and until Christian engagement with injustice is reframed from charity to justice, we can never hope to change the direction of globalization in our world. In other words, unless we begin to reverse the effects of climate change, we can expect to see an increase in the frequency and severity of storms and increased devastation as compromised ecosystems have difficulty in recovering. Likewise, until we address the extreme poverty and environmental destruction of many areas of our globe, we can expect to see more human conflicts escalate into civil war and genocide. And until we reframe the way we think about agriculture and our economy, we will continue to have serious problems with food shortages and the exploitation of labor in developing countries.

Charitable responses are a necessary aspect of a human community that is subject to social and environmental crises. The point is not that charity is bad, but that charity is not enough. The issue is one of moving people's thinking and actions from focusing exclusively on charity to considering how we are called to transform the world in ways that reflect social justice. An ethic of solidarity that arises from the moral value of mutuality moves people from a practice of doing *for* others to a practice of working *with* others. It is this shift from charity to justice that reflects a deep embrace of the value of mutuality that recognizes the sacred presence of human life in the other and that stands as the mark of the ethic of solidarity presented here.

However, addressing poverty from either the compassion stage or the responsibility stage is ultimately unable to facilitate the larger-scale process of transformation envisioned by the task of changing the direction of globalization in our world. In either case, the people that are being helped are still viewed, to some extent, as "other." As long as people primarily define their actions as helping others, either out of guilt or responsibility, they will fail to recognize the ways in which their own humanity is tied up in the health and well-being of others. As long as theological perspectives about health, wealth, and well-being are rooted in the belief that some people are "blessed" with abundance and good fortune, people are incapable of recognizing human culpability in creating a world in which people can die of starvation while food rots in fields. In fact, the ways in which Christians think theologically about hospitality, stewardship, and blessing can function to reinforce and legitimate their privilege. As long as people of wealth and privilege continue to view their abundance and prosperity as justifiable compensation or inheritance that they may choose to share with others rather than the result of social structures that perpetuate inequality, they will remain in positions of power and privilege. As long as individuals in the first world do not have to change the ways in which they live, then they are free to enjoy their privileges while assuaging their guilt and their consciences with monetary contributions or volunteer time that contributes to short-term solutions for deep-seated structural injustice. Cultivating a moral agency of mutuality encourages people to recognize the core humanity of each person while also challenging them to examine the structures of society that impoverish others (for example, lack of access to education, insufficient compensation, lack of jobs, poor nutrition, and healthcare).

These stages of moral agency are not limited to individuals. They can also offer insight into how to think more critically about community and public policy responses to issues of poverty globally and in local communities. Traditionally, the churches in the United States have a much better experience of responding to poverty with charity than justice. Homeless shelters and feeding programs certainly offer essential relief and assistance to local communities in need, but these experiences go a long way toward helping first-world Christians "feel good" without managing to change any of the underlying structures of society that contribute to the problems. The direct service aid that many churches provide is a necessary and important aspect of ministry; however, charity is not synonymous with justice. The biblical vision of social justice calls Christians to seek a transformation of social structures that will help the human community move toward sustainability and human well-being. The history of the relationship between Christians in the United States and Christians in the developing world has for too long been one of unequal power. Relationships rooted in the legacy of evangelism, missions, and charity continue to perpetuate a social inequality that mirrors and reinforces the economic inequality manifested and supported by neoliberal globalization. To the extent that these relationships remain fraught with imbalances of power due to money, education, status, or pride, these relationships fail to reflect relationships of mutuality and solidarity.

Ultimately, a moral agency of mutuality represents a new way of being in the world that offers first-world citizens a foundation for developing an ethic of solidarity as a pathway for living with integrity in a globalizing world and a model for participating in changing the direction of our world. While moral intuitions may prompt people to act, they are not static categories that define one's moral possibilities. People have the capacity to change and grow as moral agents and to embrace and develop deeper moral, philosophical, and theological resources for helping shape their lives and the structures of the world in harmony with the principles of social justice and sustainability.

Attempting to live out an ethic of solidarity is no easy task, and most people get to the place of solidarity by moving through these three stages of moral intuition—compassion, responsibility, and mutuality. Each of these stages is an important step along the journey to solidarity, and some people will stay in one of the first two stages for most of their lives. However, if people of faith truly desire to change the shape and direction that the world is headed, transformation of everyone's life is necessary.

Social ethicist Peter Paris rightly argued that it is people on the ground level, the poor themselves, who have the most capacity for change.[14] He even suggested that they may be fearful of people who come from outside offering to "help" them, and that their liberation must come from within because it is their life and death that is at stake. But it is not only *their* life and death that is at stake. While "the poor" may have the dubious advantage of recognizing the material and spiritual threats that neoliberal globalization poses, the people of the first world are also in need of transformation. What is at stake for first-world people is the ability to live our lives in ways that correspond to the most deeply held values that have been passed down through our faith traditions—the ability to live lives in ways that do not harm the earth or our neighbors, in ways that do not require that our wealth be built on the suffering of others. The problems of globalization are so dire that they require people to work together in partnership toward the common goals of social justice and sustainability in order to change the direction of globalization. Solidarity ethics offers a transformative potential for helping privileged people in the first world contribute to the transformation of the world—and the transformation of our own souls in the process.

Notes

1. Christopher Hayes, "In Search of Solidarity," *In These Times*, February 3, 2006, http://www.inthesetimes.com/main/print/2484/.

2. Hayes, "In Search of Solidarity."

3. Beverly Wildung Harrison, *Our Right To Choose: Toward a New Ethic of Abortion* (Boston: Beacon, 1983), 265, n. 20.

4. Jonathan Haidt, "The Emotional Dog and Its Rational Tail: A Social Intuitionist Approach to Moral Judgment," *Psychological Review* 108, no. 4 (2001): 814–34.

5. The rationalist school of thought in social psychology is rooted Lawrence Kohlberg's work on stages of moral development that was, in turn, based on the work of Jean Piaget.

6. Haidt, "The Emotional Dog," 817.

7. Adam Smith, *The Theory of Moral Sentiments*, ed. D. D. Raphael and A. L. Macfie (1759; repr., Oxford: Oxford University Press, 1976; repr., Indianapolis: Liberty Fund, 1982), III.3.4.

8. Haidt, "The Emotional Dog," 818.

9. Marc Parry, "Jonathan Haidt Decodes the Tribal Psychology of Politics," *Chronicle of Higher Education*, January 29, 2012.

10. Harrison, *Our Right to Choose*, 265–66, n. 20.

11. Center on Philanthropy at Indiana University, "Disaster Giving Timeline," http://www.philanthropy.iupui.edu/disaster-giving.

12. Holly Hall and Debra E. Blum, "Coming on Strong," *Chronicle of Philanthropy* 18, no. 18 (June 29, 2006): 23–27.

13. Melissa S. Brown and Patrick M. Rooney, "Giving Following a Crisis: An Historical Analysis" (Indianapolis: Center on Philanthropy at Indiana University, January 21, 2010), http://www.philanthropy.iupui.edu/files/file/crisisgivingpaper3-24-031_3.pdf.

14. Peter Paris, *The Brueggemann and Kulenkamp Lectures for Continuing Education* (unpublished lecture, Eden Theological Seminary, St. Louis, Missouri, April 1-2, 2008).

3

A Theo-Ethics of Solidarity

Over the last two hundred years, Christian ethics has offered two pathways for addressing problems of social injustice: prophetic and pragmatic. While the prophetic tradition traces its history back to the Hebrew prophets, it has more recently been associated with the Social Gospel Movement and liberation theology. In the Christian tradition, there have always been prophets who have functioned as social commentators, challenging widespread social and economic injustice and calling the people of God to accountability. From Jeremiah, Isaiah, and Micah in the Hebrew Bible to the modern-day prophets Dorothy Day and Martin Luther King Jr., prophets function to call their communities to accountability before God and they help imagine what a new world might be like. The Social Gospel Movement responded to the injustice and social inequality that resulted from the Industrial Revolution and the urbanization of US American culture by fighting for living wages, worker safety, abolishing child labor, and a shorter workweek.

Ultimately, the political and moral evil of two world wars led a new generation of theologians to reject the theology of the Social Gospel as utopian and politically naïve. One of the most influential theologians of the twentieth century, Reinhold Niebuhr, shared the Social Gospelers' emphasis on love as the starting point of Christian ethics. However, Niebuhr's understanding of love was tempered by a theological anthropology that emphasized the sinful nature of the human condition and led to the development of a more pragmatic approach to social ethics known as Christian Realism. Niebuhr was interested in social ethics and theology that had the capacity to make real social change to improve the lives of people. This pragmatism led to the development of a model of Christian ethics centered on what were called "middle axioms," which involved the articulation of moral principles that ought to guide social action and policy in the political sphere.[1] Realism dominated Protestant social ethics from the 1930s to the early 1970s, and the methodology of middle axioms has strongly influenced the way denominational and ecumenical social policies have been developed even up to the present day.[2]

In the 1960s, theologians from the developing world and from marginalized communities in the first world developed a new theological movement known as liberation theology, which takes God's act of liberating the slaves from Egypt as the starting point for thinking about God, salvation, and God's desire for life on earth. The prophetic vision of liberation from oppression and injustice that became the rallying cry of the movement hearkened back to the progressive vision of Christianity promoted by the Social Gospelers. In the early 1970s, the tension between pragmatism and prophecy was manifest in the confrontations between Christian realists, who denounced the liberationists as naïve and utopian, and the liberation theologians, who charged the realists with being "Establishment" theologians.[3]

BALANCING PROPHECY AND PRAGMATISM

All of these movements are part of the tradition of social Christianity within Protestantism that began with the Social Gospel Movement. This tradition focuses on embodying social justice by working for the democratization of economic and social power in the world. The ethic of solidarity presented here seeks to incorporate insights from all three of these significant theological movements that have shaped faith and life in the United States for the last two hundred years.

Regardless of the hermeneutic that shapes theological inquiry—whether it is hope, sin, liberation, love, or justice—a Christian ethic of solidarity will negotiate the delicate territory between pragmatism and prophetic vision. From a pragmatic perspective, it is true that a shift from neoliberal capitalism to a more just economic model of society appears to be a utopian vision, an impossibility given the political-economic structures of our present-day world. However, prophetic vision plays an important role in society by allowing people to imagine what the world *could* be like. Even if it is practically unlikely, the vision offers something to strive toward that calls people beyond the reality that they know toward a better future.

Shaped by realism, any justice ethic must recognize and acknowledge the devastation and destruction that humans have waged on one another. Seeking to understand war, terrorism, racism, prejudice, or any other form of personal or systemic violence can help people gain insight into the ways in which human behavior and attitudes contribute to the persistence of evil in the world. Possessing a deeper knowledge of human nature and human sin offers a more realistic foundation for developing strategies for social change that might be effective in establishing economic and political structures that promote peace and stability in the world. Inspired by hope, a Christian ethic of solidarity can learn from the ways in which humans have stood together to fight against oppression and offer believers the possibility of a better world. It is possible to reject the radical idealism of the Social Gospelers while retaining their fierce commitment to hope and possibility and the love that abides within the human heart—the love for children and families, for neighbors, and ultimately for a better world. Having a goal can encourage people to move forward while also helping to guide the way.

Solidarity, as defined here, is fundamentally both a theory and an action.[4] From a theoretical perspective, solidarity describes a state of being in which two or more distinct communities or groups of people develop a bond or a relationship based on a shared interest, value, or goal. When we talk about solidarity as an organizing model for changing the direction of globalization in our world, we are talking about the praxis aspect of solidarity: developing a new model for working across chasms of difference toward a common goal. Developing a deep understanding of what solidarity has to offer as a new model of thinking about and living in the world requires both theory and action. It is both a noun and a verb, a way of understanding how we can live in the world and a concrete way of living in the world.

Although the two distinct people or communities that are in solidarity may have arrived at their conclusions about the moral adequacy of the current form of globalization from radically different experiences of globalization, what matters is their shared moral assessment that the inequalities, excesses, and unsustainable nature of neoliberal globalization make it morally untenable. Solidarity is the expression of support and partnership between these two people or groups of people. It is the enactment of justice in society as a foundation for building a peace between nations and peoples that recognizes our common humanity and our common origin as beings created in God's image.

When we speak of solidarity in a globalized world, we are talking about a model of being in the world that challenges the prevailing social order. The divisions of our world are evident in the nomenclature of "first world" and "third world" that dominate political and economic discourse. These terms reflect a structured system of inequality and hierarchy that shapes the material reality of human experience. We have already detailed the ways in which the current neoliberal model of economic globalization creates situations of injustice around the world. If we understand a movement toward solidarity as a foundation from which we can facilitate a change in the direction of globalization, then we are challenged to move toward a new vision of society that is rooted in sustainability, social justice, and the transformation of the present unjust social and political order.

The starting point of a theology of solidarity is unquestionably the life and work of Jesus Christ. As the son of a carpenter raised in humble circumstances, Jesus sought out commoners from his own culture as partners in his ministry. He taught and preached in accessible public spaces and was sought after by people who were on the margins of society. He associated with and ministered to prostitutes, tax collectors, lepers, people with infirmities and disease, adulterers, madmen, soldiers, fishermen, foreigners, children, widows, rich and poor alike. Jesus walked a path of solidarity with the people of his society. He preached a message of radical social transformation in which the blind would see, the lame would walk, lepers would be healed, the deaf would hear, the dead would live again and the poor would have good news brought to them (Matt. 11:5). In this promise of a reversal of the social order of his day, Jesus offered a message of hope and good news to those who were oppressed and marginalized by social, economic, and religious structures. In proclaiming that the meek would inherit the earth (Matt. 5:5) and woe to the rich, the satisfied, and the happy (Luke 6:24-25), Jesus challenged the justice of the present social order and questioned the validity of the most powerful leaders of his own day. He came with a vision for a new world order and he practiced what he preached, living a life in true solidarity with many who were "other" in his society. His commitment to an alternative worldview and his uncompromising attitude toward seeing God's will done on earth as it is in heaven was a radical witness to a life of solidarity that can serve as a model for understanding solidarity as a contemporary Christian ethic that offers first-world Christians a pathway for living with integrity in a globalizing world.

While the Enlightenment argued that it was the human capacity to think that set us apart from the rest of the creatures in the world, scientists have documented intelligence, language, and the capacity to learn and think in a wide variety of animals, including chimpanzees and dolphins. In an age of secularism where reason and science are often pitted against faith and religion, it appears that one thing that is distinctively human is the tendency toward belief in something sacred, something that exists outside our capacity to know, something that manifests itself in beliefs, rituals, and practices that have been labeled as religion. While faith traditions, practices, beliefs, doctrines, and deities vary widely across the world's religions, there is a core experience of something sacred and true that transcends human understanding. The presence of the sacred is sometimes felt as the power of a being, deity, or force that humans feel and experience in the material world. Sometimes the presence of the sacred is felt deep inside oneself, as if in one's own heart and soul; at other times people describe the sacred as touching their lives through their relationships with other humans and God's good creation.

Despite the desires of systematic theologians throughout the ages to organize, order, and universalize human understanding of God, sin, humanity and other aspects of religious belief, all theology is subjective, particular, and bound to the social locations and material realities of particular groups of people of faith. Like the proverb of the blind people who each touched a different part of the elephant and described it as something seemingly different, different cultures and peoples who have "touched" the sacred, experience it, understand it, and describe it differently. Theology is the human attempt to understand and describe this sacred presence in light of our experience of the world in which we live.

Some people are disturbed by the idea that different people can hold different understandings of the divine and have different experiences of the sacred. They feel that truth must be spelled with a capital "T," and that unless it is universal and constant it is less than the truth. But just as the elephant doesn't change because people know it, experience it, and describe it in different ways, understanding the sacred in different ways says more about the knower than the known. Different types of knowledge (for example, scientific, artistic, emotional) change human understanding of our world. This shapes how we think, not only about our world, but about the divine as well.

In a world on the precipice of epochal change, facing an environmental crisis of our own making, what we need is a new theology for a new age—a new theology that helps to make sense of the chaotic and unjust world in which we live. A theology for people of privilege in the first world will, necessarily, be different from a theology that helps people in the developing world make sense of the world around them. This does not mean that the ultimate reality of the divine is different, just that our experiences of the world in which we live necessarily shapes our theology in distinct and meaningful ways. A theology of solidarity is a meaningful response for first-world Christians to the injustice, economic disparity, and unjust globalization that plagues our world today. If people who wish to practice an ethic of solidarity experience a real *metanoia*, there is an increased likelihood of true partnership and solidarity. The kind of worldview shift required to live out an ethic of solidarity is related to some of the most foundational aspects of theological thinking—how we understand and think about the relationship between the divine and humankind and about how we humans order our world.

Relationship between the Divine and Humankind

One of the fundamental aspects of a Christian understanding of what it means to be human is that God created us as social beings, as beings in relationship. In Genesis there are two separate creation stories that contribute to theological understanding of human nature as fundamentally relational. In the first story, found in the first chapter of Genesis, God makes all the creation: the heavens and the earth, waters and the land, night and day, birds, fish, and animals. Finally, on the sixth day, God makes humankind. Of all the aspects of the creation, only humans are declared to be made in God's image. As God creates humankind *in God's own image*, they—male and female—are created in relationship. From this creation narrative, Christians can see that one of the most sacred stories of origin understands that part of what it means to reflect the image of God is to exist in relationship with one another and with God.

The second creation story is found a few verses later, in the second chapter of Genesis. As biblical scholar Phyllis Trible has argued, in this story God makes a single, sexually undifferentiated earth creature and places the creature in the Garden of Eden.[5] Then God said, "It is not good that the earth creature should be alone." God made many living creatures to fill the garden, but none were suitable partners for the earth creature. So God caused a deep sleep to fall upon the earth creature, and from one being, God created two. It was at this point that the two beings were designated as male and female. This story demonstrates that after making the first earth creature, God recognizes that it should not be alone and God works very hard to find a suitable partner.

The important theological insight of this story is that *human beings were not intended to be alone*. Once again, relationality is a foundational assumption of Christian theological anthropology—there is something ontologically important to human personhood about living in community and caring for one another. This theme is represented throughout the biblical witness, testifying to humanity's calling to seek justice, to exhibit compassion for our neighbor, and to live in solidarity with one another. If the task of Christians is to seek the will of God and do it, then a foundational aspect of the will of God is to care for one another and to seek to establish solidarity with our neighbors, particularly in instances where we are radically estranged from them.

Solidarity is an expression of a new way of thinking about and modeling human relationships. In the neoliberal vision of humanity, humans exist as individual, autonomous beings who act solely in our own self-interest. This vision of human nature is a fundamental cornerstone of neoclassical economic theory known as *homo economicus*, a theoretical economic actor around whose expected actions economic theory is built. While it may be true that a large number of people in the world do, in fact, behave in this manner, it is not self-evident that this is an ontological aspect of our human nature, or that it is even the dominant characterization of how most humans behave.

In fact, if we examine who exactly it is that behaves this way, we find that it is predominantly people influenced by Western philosophical notions of the self that were advanced during the Enlightenment. Kant's influence on Western conceptions of human nature have become deeply embedded in the neoclassical economic theory that undergirds capitalism. Serious critiques of the adequacy of this notion of human behavior have revealed a distinct male bias in this description of how individuals make decisions.[6] Women often make decisions from within a relational matrix of competing obligations that involve the material care of others like cooking, cleaning, or caring for children or elderly relatives. Non-Western communities also often exhibit a different understanding of decision-making than the autonomous individual represented by *homo economicus,* with a stronger emphasis being placed on how decisions will impact the community.

How We Order Our World

A theo-ethic of solidarity that offers a new worldview for thinking about international relationships and globalization is deeply rooted in two fundamental theological principles that can help to guide our economic and social relationships in a transformed world. These two principles are sustainability and social justice.

SUSTAINABILITY

The principle of sustainability has become an essential ethical imperative for US Americans given the reality of our environmental impact. The environmental footprint (the amount of the earth's surface that it takes to provide everything each person uses) of the average US American is twice the average German's and about twelve times larger than the footprint of the average inhabitant of India.[7] That means that the 3.9 million babies born in the United States this year will have more than twice the impact on the earth as the 22.1 million babies born in India. Do not be fooled by the claims that it is a population explosion that is threatening the health and well-being of our planet. Equally culpable as the culprits of climate change and environmental degradation are those of us who live in societies where consumption and waste exceed the Earth's carrying capacity.

The globalization of media and the increased interaction between cultures has meant that the lifestyles of first-world people are "sold" to the developing world as the image of prosperity and wealth. While most people living in desperate poverty simply dream of food, health, and survival, many of the working poor and the middle classes in developing countries desire access to the privileges of middle-class life available in the first world. These desires are putting pressure on food and oil supplies that promise only to increase if we continue down the path of globalization that is proposed by consumer- and profit-oriented models of globalization.

It is imperative to change the direction of globalization in our world because the future of globalization and development promises to have a significant impact on the health of our planet. We live on a particular kind of planet that has a unique ability (at least as far as we know) to foster life. The carrying capacity of the Earth is finite; there are real limits to our capacity to grow and develop as a human species on this planet.[8] To gauge the potential carrying capacity of the Earth, environmentalists William Rees and Mathis Wackernagel developed the concept of the ecological footprint to measure the amount of land area necessary to support a particular lifestyle.[9] These calculations are based on the annual productivity and regenerative capacity of the earth, and they indicate that the ecological footprint of the human species outstretched the carrying capacity of the Earth in the late 1970s. By 2003, it had exceeded it by 25 percent.[10] Environmentalists acknowledge that we can manage to exceed the carrying capacity of the Earth for only so many years before we also deplete the reservoir of resources like water, oil, coal, fish, wildlife, soil, and the natural capacity of the Earth to assimilate chlorinated chemicals and carbon dioxide.

Ecological footprint calculations are based on actual usage. If we recognize that many proponents of neoliberal globalization promote the development of the world's population to match that of the first world, the potential environmental impact of over seven billion people consuming at the level of the United States must also be taken into consideration. Projections from the Global Footprint Network, which specializes in measuring the ecological footprint of various societies, warn that it would take 5.3 more planets to sustain the entire world living at the current level of US consumption.[11] Given that only 5 percent of the population currently lives in the United States and the developing nations of India and China are home to approximately 35 percent of the world's population, the way in which these countries develop will have significant ramifications for the health and well-being of our environment and its inhabitants.

However, the solution to our sustainability crisis is not simply to redirect the patterns of development in the two-thirds world. In order for the actions of first-world citizens to move to an ethic of solidarity, the basic equality of worth that exists among all people must be acknowledged. We must see the *imago Dei* that is present in each person. We cannot place more value on lives in the first world than we place on lives in the two-thirds world. We must also understand that people in the first world cannot live our lives in one way (namely, exploiting and consuming the resources of the planet) while asking or requiring people in another part of the world to live more simply. An ethic of solidarity must put into practice the fundamental belief in the shared goodness of all God's creation. From this perspective, changing the direction of globalization is not simply about people in the first world working to help those "less fortunate." Changing the direction of globalization from the standpoint of solidarity is about recognizing that the path down which we are headed is leading us to mutual disaster. The issue is not simply how we can get China and India to develop their economies in more sustainable ways. The issue is also: how do we reshape all the structures of industrial society in ways that are compatible with life on Earth? From a theological perspective, we have to recognize that this is the planet that has been entrusted to us, and we are not currently doing a very good job in caring for it.

SOCIAL JUSTICE

The most fundamental concept of the Hebrew and Christian Scriptures that pertains to thinking about the social order is the concept of social justice. Social justice, as it is presented in Scripture, demonstrates a structuring of society in ways that reflect God's concern for the well-being of all people and the created order. The social structure of Israel was designed to protect the dignity and humanity of the people by ensuring that they had access to justice.[12]

The law codes forbade lending with interest (Exod. 22:25), as it could sometimes reach as high as one-third to one-half the amount of the original loan. They also required farmers to leave crops around the edges of the field for the poor to glean (Lev. 19:9).[13] There is also particular attention in the law codes to forbidding practices that would further impoverish the poor, like the provision in Exodus that requires cloaks given as a pledge for a loan be returned before sundown because otherwise a poor person would have no covering for the night (Exod. 22:26).[14] This provision is extended in Deuteronomy, which simply prohibits the use of a widow's garment as a pledge at all (24:17).[15] The provision for social justice is not limited to people alone. There is also an understanding that social justice extends to the health and well-being of the land. In Leviticus 25, God commanded that every seventh year the land would lie fallow so that the land could rest as well.

From Isaiah to Malachi, the prophets constantly remind the people that God desires that they care for the marginalized in their midst. These are most often represented by the poor, widows, orphans, and foreigners. Archaeological evidence indicates that in the early days of Israel, the society was broadly egalitarian with no sharp divisions of income or labor.[16] It was the adoption of a monarchy, with a royal cult and culture that developed in its wake, that introduced stark divisions of class and economic inequality.[17] By the eighth century BCE and the time of the prophets Amos, Micah, and Isaiah, the disparities between the classes were enormous.[18] "Excavations at Tirzah, an early capital of the northern kingdom, show uniform houses in the tenth century, the period of Solomon. By the eighth century, some houses were mansions, and others were hovels."[19]

It is in this context that the biblical principle of *tzedakah* came to the forefront of how God was calling the Israelites to order their social and economic relationships. The Hebrew term *tzedakah*, often translated "righteousness," is a complex one that incorporates two contemporary ideas that are often at odds with one another, namely, "justice" and "charity." Rabbi Jonathan Sacks explains that the meaning of the term *tzedakah* depends on whether the person receiving a particular gesture is entitled to it.[20] This is a reflection of a social structure in which people are entitled to dignity, respect, sustenance, and care. In this context, acts of *tzedakah* that care for people in need are acts of justice rather than charity, based on a social understanding of the requirements of human dignity. In this sense, the Israelite understanding of righteousness referred to behavior that was right and just. Acts of charity, on the other hand, were gestures offered to people who were not entitled to them.

Charity, which comes from the Latin *caritas*, has come to be understood in the Christian tradition as acts of goodwill that arise out of feelings of love and kindness on the part of the actor.[21] To the extent that Jewish law understood *tzedakah* as "charity" when received by someone who was not entitled to it, contemporary US understandings of acts of charity correspond to the ancient Hebrew use of the term. However, what differs is the larger social context within which people define and understand what people are or are not "entitled" to. Rabbi Jill Jacobs argues that *tzedakah* reflected a worldview and legal system in which the powerful were responsible for the powerless, and the social structures of society were expected to be ordered in such a way as to mitigate against oppression. Sacks argues that *tzedakah* would more accurately be translated "social justice," because it reflects a Jewish understanding that "no one should be without the basic requirements of existence, and that those who have more than they need must share some of that surplus with those who have less."[22] The rights associated with justice in Hebrew society were due to each individual in the community and were meant to restore equity and harmony in the community.[23] Many of the legal codes were intended to uphold and ensure the practice of social justice, and many of the reprimands from the prophets related to the failings of the Israelites in following God's call for social justice in their relationships and in their society.

This deep sense of social justice continues in the New Testament where biblical scholar Joseph Grassi has described it as, "the equal and just distribution of economic, social, and cultural resources to all people without discrimination of any kind."[24] Social justice is the foundation of the ministry of Jesus, whose actions went beyond charity. He called for the rearrangement of the social order in which he was to bring good news to the poor, release to the captives, sight for the blind, and freedom for the oppressed (Luke 4:18). He confronted the prevailing social injustices of his time by challenging stereotypes about tax collectors and women, by challenging the legalism of the Pharisees who sought to use the law against him, and by challenging dominant notions of hierarchy and social class by redefining the way we think about family and gathering a band of followers who defied expected social norms.

God's commitment to social justice is the foundation of the exodus, in which Moses, Miriam, and Aaron lead God's people out of slavery. Christian ethicist Ed Long has argued that because the experience of the Hebrew people's liberation from Egypt shapes their identity as "Israel," liberation is the initial moral category that grounds a biblically informed ethic.[25] It is the story of the oppression and liberation of the Hebrew people and the establishment of a society based on social justice that should ground a Christian understanding of covenant relationship with God as well as the social relationships that we create on this earth. Rooting an understanding of justice in the liberating nature of God and modeling human relations and responsibilities on God's concern and passion for God's people is foundational for understanding solidarity. A Christian norm of social justice can help to guide our inquiry as we examine the current form of economic globalization and ask if it lives up to our expectations as Christians and to God's expectation for how we should order human society.

AN ETHIC OF SOLIDARITY

A theology of solidarity offers a vision of covenant and partnership between Christians in the first world and their brothers and sisters from the two-thirds world. A theology of solidarity offers hope and promise that sustainability is a more faithful and fulfilling life for Christians than consumption and prosperity. A theology of solidarity will require listening to the voices of people from the global South, it will require thinking more carefully about how our lives are bound to theirs through economic transactions in the global economy, and it is likely to require that we reshape those transactions as well as the structures of the global economy. If a theology of solidarity helps people understand how to think about living in the world, an ethic of solidarity offers a blueprint for how to live through the maintenance of four tasks—metanoia, honoring difference, accountability, and action.

METANOIA

Embracing an ethic of solidarity requires the ability to develop meaningful relationships with people across lines of difference. For many people, this will require both a new way of seeing and thinking about the world and a transformation of habits and lives. Because the lives of first-world citizens are so carefully molded, constructed, and influenced by dominant values and vision of globalization as well as dominant ideologies about poverty, development, and aid, the nurturing of a new perspective rooted in solidarity requires a radical act of *metanoia*, or transformation, of body, mind, and soul. While *metanoia* is most often translated in the New Testament as "repentance," it is more accurately understood as a total personal transformation that is reflected in both thought and behavior.[26] *Metanoia* is a radical transformation of heart, mind, and soul that literally makes one a new person. It is the word that is used to signify changes so substantial that they literally cause people to "turn around." The concept of *metanoia* does not simply refer to a spiritual experience of transformation, but suggests an accompanying transformation of behavior and lifestyle. The change that occurs is manifested in a change in how one both thinks and acts.[27] It is this kind of transformation of one's understanding of the world that is required in order for people to generate the political will to work together toward a different vision for the world. For those first-world Christians who are shaped and formed by dominant cultural attitudes and expectations about economics, development, consumerism, growth, and happiness, *metanoia* is a prerequisite for engaging in an ethic of solidarity.

An example of this use of *metanoia* comes in the third chapter of Luke, where John the Baptist proclaims a baptism of *metanoia* and goes on to challenge the crowds to "bear fruits worthy of *metanoia*" (Luke 3:8). When John is pressed by the crowds to explain what he means, he responds with very specific instructions: all of them are called to think about their positions of power and privilege and respond in ways that promote increased justice and solidarity in their community. Those who have more clothes or food than they need are instructed to share out of their abundance;[28] those who stand in positions of power (like the tax collectors) or authority (like the soldiers) are called to use their power and authority in ways that embody righteousness or right relation.[29] John's vision for the community is a vision of mutuality and justice where those with privilege are called to rethink their understanding of power in ways that promote community solidarity rather than personal aggrandizement. In a world where the benefits and attraction of being a tax collector or a soldier lay largely in the possibilities that these professions offered for getting rich through greed and exploitation, John's injunction to live righteously, take no more than their fair share, and to be satisfied with their wages was a real call to live against the cultural status quo. John's understanding of the social obligations required by justice is contextual. He does not call each person to do exactly the same thing to embody solidarity; rather, his targeted responses to different groups of people in the crowd demonstrate the ways in which people are called to think carefully and critically about their sources of power and authority and to try to determine how God is calling them to use their social position and privilege in ways that promote justice.

The experience of *metanoia* offers the possibility that people's lives can be transformed when they discover ways to embody justice and solidarity in whatever profession or vocation they have chosen. In this transformation, one experiences a turning toward God that redefines one's understanding of the purpose of life. This kind of transformation would be noticeable by the ways in which it changed the behavior (or the "fruits") of the transformed. God's call to be faithful and to practice justice wherever you are challenges people to think beyond providing charity (by meeting the immediate needs of people) to actually seeking justice, "to loose the bonds of injustice, to undo the thongs of the yoke, to let the oppressed go free" (Isa. 58:6). Communities of justice require social, economic and political structures that embody and enact justice in people's lives.

The experience of *metanoia* allows people to see the world differently and to identify the incompatibility of neoliberal globalization with the health and well-being of humankind and the planet. It is the transformative nature of *metanoia* that engenders a desire a move toward a more just social order that is consonant with God's call of how to structure society. In theological terms, this vision of global interaction can be understood as seeking to live in solidarity with our neighbors, those next door as well as those across the globe. This is no mundane version of solidarity-as-charity masquerading as a way to make people of privilege "feel good" about themselves. Solidarity is a way of describing the actions of persons and communities who seek to enact social justice in the world.

HONORING DIFFERENCE

A theory of solidarity offers a new paradigm for thinking about and understanding human behavior and human relationships. While solidarity is similar to the Christian concept of brotherhood—referring to the bonds that Christians share with one another through their common faith in God and to the political concept of *fraternité*—solidarity offers something more nuanced, more inclusive, and more useful for creating a transformational ethic for the twenty-first century. Despite the obvious objection to the patriarchal nature of the concept of "brotherhood" that is rooted in masculine identity and relationships, the concept of brotherhood also implies a negation of difference. Differences are subsumed by the bonds of family, faith, or nation that are intended to draw people together and to highlight what is shared in common rather than to expose what separates people. The concept of solidarity, on the other hand, is predicated on recognizing that differences between people not only exist, but that they are meaningful.

Before people can even hope to create relationships of solidarity that truly reflect justice, they must learn how to understand the differences that separate them. Among other things, this includes learning about differing religious traditions, cosmologies, belief systems, and habits of the heart. Understanding the ideological differences that separate people requires a deeper understanding about how those ideologies are shaped by religious practices and belief systems. If the greater goal is to achieve the kind of solidarity that reflects respect for human dignity, care of the planet, and genuine understanding of our interdependence as a human and earth community, then this requires a broad-based democratic participation of a wide representation of people in global political and economic systems and the ethical frameworks in which they are embedded.

Too often a discomfort with difference—or a fear of discord that might accompany difference—causes people to rush too quickly toward the call of brotherhood (and sisterhood), to "unity" in Christ. This problem is commonplace in contemporary churches and civil society. The appeal of unity is that it implies the absence of strife; it claims to look beyond race, gender, class, sexual orientation, and any other human characteristic that threatens division. Unity appeals because humans crave safety and harmony. When it comes down to it, many people desire for everyone to just get along.

However, the ones who often promote the status quo the loudest and the ones who avoid conflict and discord the most are often the same people who benefit from the world the way it is. It is those minority voices calling for change that are often dismissed as "troublemakers," "rabble-rousers," "dissidents," or "malcontents." Certainly, the call to unity can be compelling for the obvious reason that peace is preferable to strife, but too often the call to unity has been a tactic to suppress voices from the margin who seek to challenge the utilitarian claim that the unity of the whole is more important than the well-being of individual members of society.

A theory of solidarity that reflects an appreciation of the differences that mark human existence can offer people the opportunity to create new partnerships that recognize and respect the varied perspectives, gifts, and talents that different people bring to the task of social analysis, economic theory, and the creation of new social structures that respond to the material needs of a variety of communities of people around the world. If we can agree to join together in common cause to work toward moving society to a more sustainable and just model of globalization, then the principle of solidarity can offer a foundation for organizing our efforts as individual actors and as communities of change. Understood this way, solidarity is a postmodern concept that allows us to retain the essence of what calls to us about unity—the idea that we are joined together in common cause—while still allowing us to recognize the important differences that mark our identity and our life experience.

Solidarity implies a respect for difference in the midst of working together with others toward a common goal. It reflects a desire to maintain differences because they are uniquely important to our identity and to our common humanity. Not only are differences real, they are essential aspects of identity that shape our consciousness and our consciences in different ways. Identity politics do not dominate social and political discourse simply because they are "trendy"; they dominate discourse because people on the periphery of power—people of color, women, people with disabilities, gays and lesbians, people living in poverty, people living in the two-thirds world, people living with HIV, all sorts of people who have not historically had a recognized voice or political role in shaping politics, culture, and economic systems—have unique perspectives to offer, perspectives that help in understanding the world and its problems in new and different ways. Honoring difference will require learning how to understand and respect the lives of our global neighbors, a task that entails a good deal of listening. Democratizing our political, economic, and civil society discourses by welcoming new voices to the table brings new perspectives that help to shape public policy, economic systems, and corporate culture and behavior in new ways that are responsive to a broader set of constituencies in our world. Ultimately, the incorporation of new voices and perspectives into the discourse leads to the development of more practical, realistic, and egalitarian solutions to our collective social problems.

ACCOUNTABILITY

Beverly Harrison argued that solidarity required genuine accountability, describing it as concrete answerability to oppressed people.[30] Understood in Harrison's terms, solidarity has to be more than a sympathetic gesture in support of a cause or the pain and suffering of others. True solidarity must move beyond the wearing of a wristband or buying a T-shirt. If solidarity is to genuinely reflect accountability, it must move beyond expressions of support and into a genuine partnership with others. Solidarity implies a relationship that goes beyond a mere meeting of the minds or agreement about philosophical or even theological ideas. It represents a bond between people that calls for loyalty, compassion, and companionship, a bond rooted in the *agapē* love of the Christian tradition. Learning how to live in solidarity with one's neighbors is an expression of the Christian call to "love your neighbor as yourself" (Mark 12:31).

Certainly, it is much easier to practice this teaching if you know your neighbor, like your neighbor, or even feel kin to your neighbor in some way. This kind of provincial attitude about who counts as one's neighbor engenders a social ethic in which people can continue to care for their local community, church, and family while remaining oblivious to the ways in which their lives impact the larger world. To the extent that the United States continues to act in unilateral ways that further its own interests without regard to the perspectives, counsel, and wisdom of leaders of other nations, US Americans continue to think and act in provincial ways that distort their capacity to see people outside of the United States as their "neighbors." To the extent that Christian churches function primarily as social clubs, support groups, and havens for personal spiritual growth, people who participate in them risk further isolating themselves from the material reality of the lives of their "neighbors" who are sick, hurting, and hungry in the United States and abroad. To the extent that white Christians isolate themselves in fictive communities that reflect their own race and class positions, they live in an alienated and narcissistic world insulated, protected, and hidden from the global realities of poverty and environmental degradation that mark contemporary existence. In the Gospel of Luke, Jesus teaches in the parable of the Good

Samaritan that he expects people to see their neighbor even in those people whom they do not know and might not even like. In an era of globalization, people may not even meet the neighbors they are called to love as themselves; nevertheless, they remain our sisters and brothers, loved and cherished by God and deserving of dignity and respect.

To live out an ethic of solidarity, first-world people must get involved in some concrete engagement with oppressed or marginalized communities—locally or globally. This is important because the idea of solidarity is based on a relationship between one group that is suffering from some situation of oppression and another group that is not suffering from the oppression but acts in partnership with them or on their behalf. Botswanian New Testament scholar Musa Dube points out that "those on the dominant side are not always adversely affected by international imperialism, unless they make a conscious effort to identify with the oppressed for ethical reasons."[31] One of the foundational questions that an ethic of solidarity asks is, How is it possible for Christians to be right with God and to be right with each other and the earth when there is so much unnecessary suffering and exploitation? This is particularly important for US Christians who occupy positions of relative power and privilege vis-à-vis the poor and the marginalized peoples of the world. An ethic of solidarity thus requires that people actively engage in the building up of ties of mutuality and friendship with persons and/or communities of people who have been marginalized by their privilege.

ACTION

Denouncing neoliberal globalization as sin and working toward changing the direction of globalization requires people to live in the world in new ways. Admittedly, this is not easy work. Transforming the unsustainable consumer habits that enslave first-world communities is difficult. Restructuring systems of corporate accountability seems impossible. Developing new, sustainable, justice-oriented economic theories seems unattainable. One of the key distinguishing factors of solidarity is that it is a state of being that demands that people who are in a relationship of solidarity be willing to act on behalf of one another as a result of the bond that they share. This means that an ethic of solidarity is an ethic of action rather than simply an attitude toward others. It necessitates that individuals engage in the transformation of their own lifestyles and that they participate in changing the systems and structures of the world that create injustice. This entails the development and implementation of public policies—economic, political, and social—that establish and maintain right relationships or righteousness. It also requires individuals, families, and communities to discern together how to reshape their own lifestyles and consumer habits in ways that reflect a transformed consciousness about how to embody sustainability and justice in our daily lives.

As people contemplate what change might look like in their personal lives, new ways of imagining daily life can begin to challenge deeply embedded cultural expectations: What would life be *like* without a television? Without meat? Without a two-story brick home in the suburbs? Without a high-paying job? Without the latest fashions in my closet? Without McDonald's or Coca-Cola or Walmart? Many people fear that the change that is required is so radical that they will lose something important, something that seems essential to life, something they do not want to give up.

However, perhaps this fear is misplaced. Maybe a better starting point is to ask to what extent increased consumerism has made people "happier." Psychologists who study life satisfaction have documented that while the average person's income in the United States more than doubled between 1957 and 2002, the percentage of people who reported themselves as "very happy" remained constant at around 30 percent.[32] If that's the case a better set of questions might be: What would my life be like if I worked toward decreasing my environmental impact on the world? What would my life be like if I lived sustainably? What would my life be like if I lived it in solidarity with people in the two-thirds world? What would my life be like if I took a job that contributed toward solving the problems of economic and environmental globalization rather than a job that contributed to them? What would the United States look like if Christians demanded these things? What would the world look like if all people of faith began to demand these things? Thinking about the ways in which building lives of solidarity might offer deeper and more meaningful vocational opportunities as well as personal satisfaction is a more positive way to approach the lifestyle changes that will be required in developing sustainable economies and just societies.

While the lifestyle changes that accompany solidarity are necessary for changing the direction of globalization in our world, it is important to also recognize that the health and well-being of our world is not anyone's *individual* responsibility. As important as individual behavior is, the problems of poverty, environmental degradation, and inequality in our world cannot be solved simply by individual lifestyle choices. Individual behavioral transformation is a necessary but insufficient condition for changing the direction of globalization. The larger challenges that face us as a human community require a concerted effort at systemic transformation. While the choices people make as individual consumers are important, individual consumer behavior must be examined within the context of the global market economy in which it is exercised. Economic justice is, at its heart, an issue of systemic transformation that requires a careful look at how we have theorized and structured our economies. An ethic of solidarity requires people to be engaged in working toward structural change in society.

CONCLUSION

The task of changing the direction of where we are headed as a global community is not simply a call for a new direction for public policy in our world; it is also a radical call for people living in the first world to change the direction that their own lives are headed. And getting to a place where we are able to join together with our compatriots in the two-thirds world in ways that move us toward a true partnership that honors each of our unique gifts and strengths is a journey that requires much work. For first-world citizens, developing relationships of solidarity across lines of difference requires acknowledging complicity in contemporary forms of globalization and examining the forms of privilege that shape life in the developed world.

Notes

1. Dennis McCann, *Christian Realism and Liberation Theology: Practical Theologies in Creative Conflict* (Maryknoll, NY: Orbis, 1981), 93.

2. Ronald Preston, "Middle Axioms," in *Dictionary of Christian Ethics*, ed. James F. Childress and John Macquarrie (Philadelphia: Westminster, 1986), 382.

3. For a detailed analysis of this debate, see McCann, *Christian Realism and Liberation Theology*.

4. Ada Maria Isasi-Diaz makes a very similar claim in her important article on the topic, "Solidarity: Love of Neighbor in the 1980s," in *Feminist Theological Ethics: A Reader*, ed. Lois K. Daly (Louisville: Westminster John Knox, 1994), 77–87.

5. Phyllis Trible's essay, "A Love Story Gone Awry," argues that the original Hebrew poetry has been misunderstood and mistranslated within patriarchal religious traditions. Trible argues that *adam* is a Hebrew word that means "earth creature" and that it is not until the second creature is created woman, *ishshah*, that the first creature becomes man, *ish*. See Trible, "A Love Story Gone Awry," in *God and the Rhetoric of Sexuality* (Philadelphia: Fortress Press, 1978), 72–143.

6. For an excellent analysis of the gender bias of economic "rationality" and the inadequacy of neoclassical economics, see Carol Robb, "Rational Man and Feminist Economists on Welfare Reform," in *Welfare Policy: Feminist Critiques*, ed. Elizabeth M. Bounds et al. (Cleveland: Pilgrim, 1999), 77–94.

7. Jason Venetoulis, Dahlia Chazan, and Christopher Gaudet, *Ecological Footprint of Nations 2004*, Redefining Progress, http://www.globalchange.umich.edu/globalchange2/current/labs/ecofoot/footprintnations2004.pdf, p. 12.

8. Donella Meadows, Jorgen Randers, and Dennis Meadows, *Limits to Growth: The 30-Year Update* (White River Junction, VT: Chelsea Green, 2004).

9. Brian Halweil et al., *State of the World 2004* (New York: W.W. Norton, 2004), 291–92.

10. World Wildlife Fund, *Living Planet Report 2006* (Gland, Switzerland: World Wildlife Fund, 2006), 2.

11. Victoria Johnson and Andrew Simms, *Chinadependence: The Second UK Interdependence Report* (London: New Economics Foundation, 2007), table 4, 21.

12. For an overview of the concept of social justice in the Hebrew Bible, see Bruce V. Malchow, *Social Justice in the Hebrew Bible* (Collegeville, MN: Liturgical Press, 1996).

13. Ibid., 23.

14. Ibid.

15. Ibid.

16. Ibid., 10–11.

17. Ibid., 11.

18. Ibid., 12.

19. Ibid.

20. Jonathan Sacks, *The Dignity of Difference: How to Avoid the Clash of Civilizations* (New York: Continuum, 2002), 113–15.

21. Jill Jacobs, *There Shall Be No Needy: Pursuing Social Justice Through Jewish Law and Tradition* (Woodstock, VT: Jewish Lights Publishing, 2010), 43.

22. Ibid., 114.

23. Malchow, *Social Justice in the Hebrew Bible*, 16.

24. Joseph A. Grassi, *Informing the Future: Social Justice in the New Testament* (Mahwah, NJ: Paulist, 2003), 1.

25. Edward LeRoy Long, *To Liberate and Redeem: Moral Reflections on the Biblical Narrative* (Cleveland: Pilgrim, 1996), 12.

26. J. P. Louw and Eugene A. Nida, eds., *Greek-English Lexicon of the New Testament Based on Semantic Domains*, 2nd ed., vol. 1 (New York: United Bible Societies, 1989), 510.

27. Ibid.

28. "Whoever has two coats must share with anyone who has none; and whoever has food must do likewise" (Luke 3:11).

29. To the tax collectors he said, "Collect no more than the amount prescribed for you" (Luke 3:13), and to the soldiers, "Do not extort money from anyone by threats or false accusation, and be satisfied with your wages" (Luke 3:14).

30. Beverly Wildung Harrison, "Theological Reflection in the Struggle for Liberation," in *Making the Connections: Essays in Feminist Social Ethics*, ed. Carol S. Robb (Boston: Beacon, 1985), 244.

31. Musa Dube, "Postcoloniality, Feminist Spaces, and Religion," in *Postcolonialism, Feminism, and Religious Discourse*, ed. Laura Donaldson and Kwok Pui-lan (New York: Routledge, 2002), 102.

32. State of the World 2004, NY: W. W. Norton, 2004, 166.

4

Moving Toward Solidarity

For people of privilege, one of the first steps in moving into an ethic of solidarity is to come to terms with their own privilege. The challenge of this task is that it requires people to acknowledge aspects of their identity and social location from which they benefit. This can be a difficult task in a culture where very few people think of themselves as privileged, wealthy, or powerful. In fact, the majority of people in the United States classify themselves as "middle class," even many of those who fall in the upper 20 percent income bracket (>US $100,066).[1] For the 1.29 billion people in the world who live on less than $1.25 US dollars a day, that fact is quite remarkable.[2] What becomes obvious is that wealth has both absolute and relative qualities to it. People in the United States often think about wealth in absolute terms.

Popular perceptions of what it means to be wealthy in the United States relate to those people who can afford to buy or do whatever they want, whenever they want.[3] In a recent survey of US investors conducted by UBS, a global financial services firm, 50 percent of respondents defined "wealth" as not having any financial constraints. For these people, wealth is defined as the point at which money is simply not a factor in one's decision-making processes. Only 31 percent of the millionaires in the survey considered themselves "wealthy," and $5 million was the threshold at which the majority of respondents (60 percent) began to indicate that they considered themselves "wealthy." For better or worse, most people think of themselves as people who *do* have to think about money, and most people who have to think about money define themselves as "middle class." Most people have to plan for their retirement, save to buy a new car, a new house, or to go on vacation. They have to make budgets and stick to them in order to cover their expenses, regardless of their income level. However, from the vantage point of the majority of people in the two-thirds world or even from the perspective of people in poverty within the first world, wealth is relative. New cars, new houses, and vacations are not even on their radar screens. The wants and needs of people who live on the margins of society are much more basic: healthy food to eat, a clean, safe place to live, and opportunities for jobs that pay a living wage. Perspective makes all the difference when examining the different material circumstances of people around the world.

In a cultural climate where people who are clearly wealthy by any objective measure nevertheless identify as "middle class," it is extremely difficult to discuss aspects of privilege and the ways in which privilege shapes wealth, inequality, poverty and justice in society. The three most prominent forms of privilege—race, class, and gender—are unearned and largely immutable. While a relatively small number of people will change their gender, and some may pass as a different race, class is the category that is most often touted as a changeable aspect of identity. In fact, a 2005 New York Times poll found that 80 percent of US Americans believe it is possible to pull yourself up by your bootstraps.[4] This belief is reinforced by the examples of people like Oprah Winfrey who have achieved iconic status in our culture and Horatio Alger's stories about people who have remarkable experiences of social mobility. Much of the mythology and history of the United States is grounded in the promise of the American Dream that political freedom offers the possibility of prosperity and upward mobility for people, regardless of their class status. While social mobility is certainly *possible* in the United States, studies show it is not *likely*. One recent study showed that a son whose father made $16,000 a year (putting him in the lowest 10 percent of wage earners) had only a 5 percent chance of earning over $55,000.[5] While the mythology of the American Dream ostensibly gives hope to poor and working-class people that wealth, stardom, and fame are within reach for those who are talented and hardworking, the prominence of rags-to-riches stories can also function as a cultural narrative to blame the poor for *not* working hard enough. Rather than examining the social factors that contribute to increased inequality and lack of social mobility, individuals are often blamed for not working hard enough to move themselves out of poverty.

Issues of race, class, and gender are three of the most volatile topics in contemporary US society. Fifty years of civil rights, women's rights, and union activism have led many people who are privileged to believe that we have addressed inequality in the United States. Too often issues like affirmative action, reparations for slavery, pay equity, living wage, and other social justice campaigns are dismissed as activities of special interest groups and tactics of divisive identity politics. But privilege is not limited to race, class, and gender. People enjoy many different kinds of privilege associated with factors like age, sexual orientation, physical ability, ethnicity, nationality, and religion.[6]

One of the things that makes privilege tricky is that it is often invisible to the people who possess it. Like the air that we breathe, most people don't think about how the world works unless it does not work for them in some way. Most white, non-Hispanic people in the United States expect that if they are well-dressed and behave politely, they will be generally respected in public, they will be waited on in restaurants and stores, and that law enforcement exists to protect them. These expectations are reasonable and hardly regarded as "privileges" by the people who hold them; rather, they are simply reflections of their experience of how the world "works."

Even more importantly, there is nothing wrong with these expectations. In fact, all people ought to be able to expect this kind of treatment as recognition of their basic humanity. However, these expectations are not shared equally throughout US society. Prejudice against people who do not conform to a society's norms is often imperceptible to the people in the majority culture, but it shapes the lives of minority people, their families, and their communities in meaningful ways. Muslim women who wear head scarves in the United States often experience a lack of public respect for their choice. Many African-Americans have related their experiences of being ignored in restaurants and stores, or worse, even followed to make sure they are not stealing. And the reality of racial profiling by police departments in the United States demonstrates that the expectation that law enforcement is there to protect law-abiding citizens is not universally shared. In societies that are plagued by prejudices of race, class, and gender, basic human rights have become "privileges" afforded to people with the "right" skin color, education, gender, or checkbook balance.

In her influential essay on "white privilege," Peggy McIntosh points out that some aspects of privilege, like expecting your neighbors to be decent to you or not having your race count against you in court, should be basic norms in society.[7] The fact that they are not reflects a serious injustice in the social structure of society that confers basic human rights on a select group of citizens in a way that privileges or gives advantage to that group over against other groups of people. It is this kind of systemic organization of privilege that leads to an unequal distribution of power in society and the ability of the powerful to abuse those with less power and privilege. McIntosh also points out that other privileges, like the ability to ignore less powerful people, can distort the humanity of both those who exercise that privilege and those who are slighted.[8]

Privilege is complicated. For those who benefit from some forms of privilege, it does not always mean that their lives are easy. Natural disasters, physical illness, and accidents do not acquiesce to the social privileges that humans have constructed. Talk about privileges of race, class, and gender can often be particularly difficult for people who might have access to one kind of privilege (for example, white race privilege) yet are poor or working class, or people of wealth and social status who are also members of a minority religion or race. In those circumstances, it often feels as if one does not have any social privilege.

Additionally, people often consider aspects of their privilege earned or simply the result of hard work on their part and not really a privilege at all. Education, for instance, is earned in the sense that individuals must work hard to learn the material and do well in school. Education is not something that is given away or that is inheritable. With that said, the quality of and access to educational experiences can vary widely in ways that are related to privilege. Universal access to education is an important aspect of addressing poverty and equipping people with the knowledge and skills necessary to live healthy and meaningful lives. However, the quality of that education also matters, and people with various forms of privilege can often gain access to higher-quality education or even advantages of prestige or contacts that come with attending particularly prominent schools.

Many people also consider their wealth as something that they earned through their hard work and diligence—first as students and then as successful employees who make a good living and spend their money wisely and prudently. While it is true that people who work hard ought to be paid well for their time and effort, the problem with this narrative is that focuses only on what the individual has done (or thinks they have done) by themselves, without recognizing the ways in which structures of privilege may have contributed to their success and ultimately to their wealth. It also fails to account for why there are so many poor people who work very hard at low-paying jobs that fail to compensate them in ways that allow independence, self-sufficiency, and access to "the good life."

Recent controversies in South Africa illustrate the danger of focusing too much on the trope of "hard work and enterprise" as the foundations of wealth and success.[9] Despite the well-documented structural benefits that apartheid offered to whites over black and colored South Africans—including jobs that were reserved for whites, land that was taken from blacks and given to whites, government subsidies for white farmers, and higher quality education for white children, just to name a few—the FW de Klerk Foundation rejected the notion of white privilege as a meaningful tool of social analysis in a 2011 statement that claimed, "A substantial proportion of whites cannot be described as being 'privileged' at all. The vast majority have acquired whatever wealth they have through the same means as their counterparts throughout the rest of the world: through hard work and enterprise."[10] The point of examining various forms of privilege is not to deny that those who hold that privilege are good and hardworking people as individuals. Rather, the point is to explore the ways in which structures of society are sometimes shaped to benefit (or "privilege") some at the expense of others.

Christian ethicist Mary Hobgood has pointed out that one of the most insidious aspects of privilege is precisely the way that people have been socialized to understand their own privilege as a "just reward for superior talent and effort" and to see "disadvantage as a result of individual inadequacies."[11] The inability to see one's own privilege can make it difficult to engage in meaningful social analysis that enables first-world citizens to see the ways in which their wealth and privilege are important factors in understanding economic globalization in the world. For people who hold privilege, part of the ethical task is to evaluate which privileges ought to be universal moral norms and which privileges might be distorting our humanity.

Enlightenment attitudes of liberalism shape dominant social attitudes in the United States in ways that promote individualism, independence, and self-sufficiency. In such a culture, it is common for people to blame the poor for their situation and to chastise them for not working harder to lift themselves out of poverty. The economic, political, and military dominance of the United States in the current era of neoliberal globalization means that these same liberal attitudes are often active in shaping public policy responses to the crisis of poverty internationally. While there have always been differences between the wealth of nations, the crippling poverty that many people in the two-thirds world face is a result of patterns of social, economic, and political behavior over the last several hundred years that have functioned to *impoverish* people in the developing world. These experiences of colonialism, racism, and economic globalization are rooted in patterns of elitism, authoritarianism, and exploitation that have led to a world of vast inequalities between nations and between upper and lower classes within nations.

While it is true that poor people, like people anywhere, sometimes make bad choices, choices that may even contribute to their problems, the primary contributing factors that lead to poverty are not laziness, apathy, or low intelligence. Rather, poverty is primarily a result of historical circumstances, political decisions, and economic systems.[12] It is imperative to include a serious examination of the history of colonialism, racism, and empire in any critical analysis of globalization because the current crises and injustices have deep roots in exploitation and marginalization that trace back centuries. No adequate approach to addressing these problems can be developed without understanding how they developed and how countries in the global North contributed significantly to the problems that people in the developing world are facing. Certainly, class, race, and gender oppression are not inventions of the modern era, as humans have long been inclined to use power and status to build themselves up at the expense of others. Nevertheless, the specific problems of inequality and poverty that we face in our world today are directly related to the exploitation of the developing world by the developed countries over centuries.

A History of Building Privilege in the United States

Paying attention to privilege requires that people examine the historical developments that have led to the present structures of our political economy and our global world order. Remembering social history can help people see the ways in which social problems in their communities are sometimes the result of public policy decisions that have functioned to impoverish and disenfranchise marginalized members of their community. This history helps people understand how forms of injustice have been "institutionalized" in our society. This institutionalization of injustice is also known as structural injustice, and is manifested in patterns of unjust policies that disproportionately impact particular groups of people in ways that further marginalize, exclude, and disenfranchise whole groups and classes of people. Examining this history is the first step in a process of framing an understanding of the social problems of poverty, inequality, and environmental crisis in ways that will help develop viable strategies of social transformation rooted in justice and sustainability. In addition to understanding the structural aspects of economic injustice, building solidarity with people who have been harmed by this system also requires first-world people to take stock of how privilege has shaped their lives.

Understanding privilege in the United States accurately necessitates a consideration of the history of prejudice within its borders. While people are often taught about the ways in which prejudice disadvantages particular groups of people, they are often not challenged to consider the ways in which that prejudice may work to their own advantage through the creation of privilege.[13] Basically defined, a privilege is a right or an advantage that some people have that is not available to everyone in the society. The benefits of privilege are often so deeply woven into our experience of reality that people who hold them do not recognize the unequal distribution of these factors in our society. Nor do they always recognize the ways in which privilege is linked to inequality and how both have shaped the economic and social development of our country. Examining how structures of privilege were built into our social contract and our political economy is a necessary step in understanding the complex moral problems associated with contemporary economic globalization.

This task begins with recognizing and acknowledging the native peoples who occupied North America prior to the European invasion in the fifteenth and sixteenth centuries. The colonies that are sometimes referred to as the "neo-Europes" (United States, Canada, Australia, New Zealand/Aotearoa) share a different kind of colonial heritage from the colonies located in Africa, Asia, and Latin America. Each of the neo-Europes shares the dubious distinction of having established majority "white" populations that effectively decimated and displaced original indigenous populations. From an estimated ten million Native peoples residing in North America prior to European contact, by 1900 the number was closer to three hundred thousand.[14]

The systematic destruction of the indigenous populations of Native Americans occurred through warfare, massacre, disease, and forced migration. This genocide was not only supported by the Protestant and Catholic colonizing countries but also often mandated by church hierarchies and supported by the dominant theological perspectives that portrayed the North American continent as a gift from God to the Christian conquerors. Indeed, one Puritan leader remarked after the Pequot War in which nearly a thousand Native Americans were killed, "Thus was God pleased to smite our enemies and to give us their land as an inheritance."[15] This type of conquest theology is a central aspect of a colonial and imperialistic mentality that continues to fuel dualistic divisions between groups of people when one group claims that "God is on our side" as a way to justify acts of aggression and power. Remnants of this type of theology were evident in the original name, "Operation Infinite Justice," for the US attack on Afghanistan following 9/11. The name was changed after Muslim and Christian leaders challenged that it was an inappropriate elision of the roles of God and the state.[16]

There are also deep and historic connections between Christian imperialism and economic prosperity that help to contextualize the economic globalization and Western imperialism that mark our current era.[17] Historian Mary Sawyer points out that while it is true that English colonists came seeking religious liberty, the promise of economic security and the acquisition of land and other resources were "an equal if not more powerful incentive."[18] Furthermore, the Spanish conquistadors came primarily seeking wealth through the procurement of land, resources, and new subjects. The Spanish also brought with them a belief that it was the duty of the state to evangelize and convert to Catholicism all those with whom they came into contact. Indeed, it was the Spanish crown that "appointed bishops and religious superiors, decided what priests would come to the New World, paid the salaries of the clergy, and created new dioceses."[19]

An examination of the attitudes and behavior of the majority of white Christians during the slave trade in the United States reveals a picture that is little better. African slaves and their descendants were denied basic human rights and human dignity by Christian slave apologists, who argued that "Black people were not members of the human race."[20] Womanist social ethicist Katie Cannon documents that this position was justified through the biblical story of Ham, who was identified as "the progenitor of the Black race." [21] In the story, Ham, who is one of Noah's sons, sees his father naked after he has passed out from drinking too much wine. Ham tells his brothers, Shem and Japheth, what he has seen and Shem and Japheth cover their father. When Noah learns of Ham's behavior, he curses Ham's son, Canaan, proclaiming that Canaan will become a "slave of slaves" to his brothers (Gen. 9:25).

Mistranslation, scribal errors, and faulty interpretations of the text led to two dominant beliefs that influenced the way that many Christians, Jews, and Muslims thought about slavery in the eighteenth and nineteenth centuries. First, the identities of father and son, Ham and Canaan, were elided to the point that the tradition assigns Noah's curse to Ham rather than his son. Second, a tradition developed that associated Ham and his descendants with people of African descent.[22] These beliefs contributed to religious justifications of the enslavement of Africans by Christians, Jews, and Muslims, who shared the book of Genesis as a sacred text.[23]

Furthermore, white Christians defended the institution of slavery by appeal to biblical passages that supported and justified slavery. Particularly influential were texts from Leviticus and passages from the New Testament books Luke, Peter, Timothy, Philemon, and Titus. The Leviticus passage describes the appropriate ways of obtaining slaves "from the nations around you," and declared that slaves could be passed down to descendants as inherited property (Lev. 25:44-46).[24] The New Testament passages demonstrate a cultural acceptance of the practice of slavery in the early Christian period and even instruct slaves to obey their masters and to accept their servitude.

Slavery was also justified by Christian claims that slave traders and slave owners "saved poor, degraded, and wretched African peoples from spiritual darkness."[25] The same colonial patterns of racial, intellectual, and moral superiority that white Christians demonstrated in their attitudes toward Native peoples were evident in their attitudes and actions toward black slaves and their descendants. While many Christian pro-slavery advocates believed that slaves bore the "curse of Ham" and were destined to servitude, their paternalism also allowed them to believe that slavery was in the best interest of the slaves since their masters baptized them into the Christian religion and offered them access to salvation through knowledge of Jesus Christ. Historian David Brion Davis quotes a prominent agricultural reformer as saying that "the excesses of his [Negro's] animality are kept in restraint and he is compelled to lead an industrious, sober life, and certainly a more happy one than he would if he was left to the free indulgences of his indolent savage nature."[26]

There is a popular sentiment in the United States that emancipation and the Civil Rights Movement solved the "problem" of race in our country by freeing slaves and providing them with equal access to civil rights. Since the election of Barack Obama, many people have begun to refer to the United States as a "postracial" society, a term that indicates we have moved beyond prejudice and racism to a point of a broad-based social equality. Another way that the term "postracial" is used is akin to the idea of "colorblindness," meaning that people simply do not notice the race of others because it is not important.[27] In her book *The New Jim Crow: Mass Incarceration in the Age of Colorblindness,* legal scholar Michelle Alexander identifies the trend toward embracing "colorblindness" as the root cause of the mass incarceration of black people in the United States.[28]

Many of the people who affirm the notion of "colorblindness" consequently attribute contemporary social crises in black America, including the disproportionate number of black people living in poverty, serving time in jail, and dropping out of school, to the attitude and "nature" of blacks. Oftentimes the language that is used is frighteningly similar to the offensive racist rhetoric that was prominent in arguments over slavery and the "nature" of African slaves and their descendants.[29] In order to understand the contemporary situation of black US Americans, it is necessary to examine what happened to black citizens after emancipation and to see how racial prejudice was embedded in the structures of society in ways that continued to disenfranchise and discriminate against black people.

While the brief era of Reconstruction attempted to enfranchise newly freed black Americans and set up some semblance of justice, the racism and prejudice in the South won the day as new political, social, and economic structures were constructed in ways intended to keep black people "in their place." Sharecropping arrangements that allowed poor black and white farmers to work the land as tenant farmers were so exploitative that they ensured the continued indebtedness (and poverty) of the farmers. While the Fifteenth Amendment made it legal for black men to vote, eleven Southern states created poll taxes and literacy requirements that effectively disenfranchised most African-Americans.

Racial segregation was assured through the implementation of "Jim Crow" laws that created parallel social spaces for blacks and whites (for example, schools, restaurants, water fountains, toilets) that were always separate, but never equal. As the population of blacks increased in Northern cities during the Great Migration (1910–1929) and the Second Great Migration after World War II, segregation and discrimination also increased in other parts of the country. Blacks were often denied housing loans through the practice known as "redlining," which used red lines to mark areas on city maps that lenders considered "hazardous." Not surprisingly, many of the areas deemed "hazardous" had high black populations. Redlining made home ownership for blacks, and consequently the economic development of black neighborhoods, extremely difficult. Racist attitudes of white homeowners made it nearly impossible for blacks to buy homes in white neighborhoods. In some Northern communities in the 1920s, community groups calling themselves "neighborhood improvement associations" formed in white neighborhoods with the intention of keeping blacks from moving into their areas.[30]

Blacks were also largely excluded from Roosevelt's New Deal, which did not provide domestic and agricultural workers with unemployment and Social Security benefits at a time when two-thirds of blacks were in these occupations.[31] African-American veterans returning from World War II also had more difficulty than their white counterparts in accessing the benefits of the G.I. Bill due to the practice of redlining and the racial prejudice against blacks that permeated the whole country (including the V.A. and educational institutions). While minority communities have always tended to settle in residential enclaves, they usually integrate into the larger social landscape within a generation or two. The practice of racial segregation made this impossible for African-Americans and led to a concentration in population density of black communities in Northern cities that reached 90 percent by 1950.[32]

The urban renewal programs of the 1960s and 1970s, which were intended to revitalize downtown areas, effectively decimated these communities by tearing down inner-city housing and moving the poorest and most vulnerable residents into new public housing "projects."[33] One major problem with this approach was the fact that only one unit was built for every ten destroyed. A second was that this social experiment destroyed the core identity of these communities, which had previously been neighborhoods with high social capital and informal networks, where affluent, middle-class, working-class, and poor blacks lived side by side.[34]

Similar examples of imperial behavior and racist public policy can be found in the histories of numerous immigrant and minority groups in the United

States. People often forget that large numbers of US citizens of Hispanic descent did not immigrate to this country but found their citizenships transferred after the Mexican-American War.[35] This has been described as a war of aggression on the part of the United States, part of the policy of "Manifest Destiny" that held that Euro-Americans had been given this land by God and it was their destiny to conquer and control it. The Chinese Exclusion Act of 1882 was the only immigration law that specifically excluded a group of people as immigrants based on race. People of Japanese descent were locked up in internment camps during World War II, including many who were US citizens. Anti-miscegenation laws that prevented interracial marriages were used in many states to prevent various minorities from "mixing" with the white race.

There were certainly people of all races and ethnicities who fought against the injustice of each of these measures in their own day. Furthermore, much progress has been made in breaking down statutory injustice and addressing social inequality in the United States. Legalized segregation is over, and civil rights laws have guaranteed equal access to public spaces and public services. The Americans with Disabilities Act legislated against discrimination for people with disabilities and has prompted increased physical access to public spaces. Apologies and reparations have been made to Japanese Americans who were interned during World War II. Gay rights are increasing in many parts of the country, and more and more LGBTQI (lesbian, gay, bisexual, transgender, queer, intersex) people are coming out and openly acknowledging their preferred sexual orientation and gender identity and expression. There has been an increased attention to issues of diversity and inclusiveness, and the personal attitudes and actions of many people have changed.[36]

While it is true that the United States has made great strides in addressing institutionalized racism in our country, prejudice and discrimination still function to shape public policy, political opinion, and corporate America in ways that reinforce existing race and class privilege. The immigration debate in the US, for instance, continues to reflect mean-spirited and demeaning attitudes about particular sets of immigrants who are singled out for derision and persecution. While asylees and refugees who enter this country legally are offered support and resettlement assistance, many economic refugees from Latin America are commonly referred to as "illegals." The presence of undocumented workers who enter the country outside of official channels is certainly against the law; however, referring to human beings as "illegals" strips them of their humanity. Even if their actions are against the law, it is the activity that they engaged in that is against the law, not their very status as a human person. Rhetoric like this functions to strip away the humanity of undocumented workers and contributes to the general public's attitude toward an entire ethnic group of immigrants. There are many different ways that people can become undocumented in the United States. This happens when people cross the border illegally, but it also happens when student, tourist, or work visas expire before people leave the country. However, the term "illegals" most often refers to undocumented Hispanic immigrants, making it akin to an ethnic slur.

Racial and ethnic prejudice in our country cannot be glossed over as simply an unfortunate aspect of our history. Disproportionate incarceration rates of blacks, immigration enforcement policies that target Hispanics, and higher mortality rates for cancer in black patients suggest that daily life in the United States is different for different groups of people based on the color of their skin. The economic disparity between white, black, and Hispanic households is another sharp indication that the United States is not a level playing field. According to the most recent statistics from the US Census Bureau, the rate of homeownership in the United States is 66 percent; the median income in 2009 was $49,777;[37] and life expectancy was seventy-eight.[38] If we disaggregate the data for net worth according to race, we discover that the median net worth for white households in 2007 was estimated at $170,400, while the figure for non-white/Hispanic households was $27,800.[39] The Economic Policy Institute estimates that in 2009 the median net worth of Hispanic households was $6,325, black households was $5,677, and white households, $113,149.[40] These numbers shed important light on enduring economic and racial disparities in our country, and they help to identify who has access to the life of "prosperity" that is promoted as part of the "American Dream." While the task of social ethics requires engaging in historical social analysis that acknowledges the ways in which privilege has been woven into the structures of social and economic relationships and systems, it is also necessary to examine the way that privilege functions to benefit (and harm) individuals within those systems.

Recent research on prejudice and race indicates that most racism in our culture is no longer as overt as it used to be. Psychologist John Dovidio of Yale notes that while conscious prejudice has declined, unconscious prejudice has remained steady.[41] Dovidio and his colleagues refer to this unconscious prejudice as "aversive racism." This phenomenon helps to explain decades of experiments simulating hiring decisions between equally qualified candidates of different races in which the white candidate is recommended for the job more often than the black candidate with equal credentials.[42] While these same experiments indicate that there is no discrimination in cases where one candidate's qualifications are clearly superior, when the case is close and reasonable arguments could be made for either candidate, racial prejudice unconsciously influences decision making.[43]

For people who live in a culture with a deep history of institutional racism, it is difficult to know how people's psyches have been shaped by the prejudices that permeate daily life and the histories and stories of different families and communities. In these circumstances, critical examination of how people's consciences are shaped with regard to race, class, and gender is a significant aspect of self-understanding, particularly regarding the privileges that one enjoys.

BUILDING RELATIONSHIPS

Poverty, inequality, and environmental degradation are neither inevitable nor necessary. Human communities construct the societies in which we live—with all of their economic, social, and cultural conditions. Studying our history is important because it can help us to understand the present in more realistic and useful ways. Knowing the ways in which our social and economic policies have functioned to institutionalize injustice can help us gain clarity regarding what must be done to dismantle the structures of injustice that contribute to poverty, inequality, and environmental degradation. It is possible to shape our world in different ways and the health and well-being of our communities ought to reflect the values and commitments of those communities.

The point of owning our past and recognizing our various privileges is not to engender guilt. While guilt may be an appropriate and necessary first step in the process of developing relationships of solidarity across lines of difference and privilege, too often guilt functions in a paralyzing and disabling way. Shame and regret do nothing to establish God's vision of right relation and justice in the world. Christians believe that the good news of the gospel is that people can be forgiven for their sins through God's unending grace. Following the teachings of Christ offers people the opportunity to participate in the transformation of the world, working as God's hands and feet here on the ground.

But God's gift of grace does not free people to simply continue to live their lives as they always have. While God freely offers forgiveness for sins, people are challenged to go and sin no more. In so doing, sometimes people are called to change their lives and the oppressive structures in which they live in order to heed God's call. While people are not culpable for the injustices that are part of their nation's history, nor for the unjust actions of their ancestors, they are responsible for how they respond to history and how they act in the world to change the trajectories of injustice that continue to oppress and marginalize people. In much the same way, people are not responsible for the unearned privileges they receive in society based on skin color, gender, sexual orientation, or other circumstances of birth. However, people are responsible for recognizing the ways in which they receive social benefits that they have not earned and in working toward the transformation of social structures that confer differential benefits on people in unjust ways.

Too often, in assessing social structures and issues of poverty and inequality, attention is focused solely on poor people and trying to figure out how to help them get out of poverty. While this is a necessary and even essential element of crafting useful social policy, what are too often overlooked are the inequalities in the social structures that function to reinforce the class positions and wealth generation of the upper-middle and upper classes. While assumptions are often made about the brilliance, hard work, and merit of wealthy people, in fact many upper-middle class and wealthy people benefit from education, connections, financial support, economically stable home environments—in essence, unearned privileges.

The ways in which white Christians in the United States have structured their lives so that they do not know the devastating reality of poverty and injustice in this country, much less in many parts of the two-thirds world, are a direct consequence of a heritage of exploitation, privilege, and prosperity. By wiping out the majority of Native peoples and moving the rest to remote reservations located on land deemed undesirable by the US government, white US Americans have created a fictive expression of society that is majority white. By fleeing the inner-city and urban areas of our country over the last several decades as minority families moved in, white US Americans have attempted to re-create white and/or wealthy enclaves of "normalcy" and "safety." In these places whites retain power, authority, and control over their businesses, their social lives, and the lives and experiences of their children.

To the extent that any group can isolate itself from the diversity of peoples and life experiences in our world; to the extent that the white majority continue to create and recreate social worlds of white privilege and power; to the extent that capitalist economic systems require the exploitation of wage labor in order to turn a profit; to the extent that white people in the United States continue to prosper disproportionately to minority peoples in their communities and to most of the rest of the world's people, our heritage and identity as people of faith is tragically misshapen, distorted, and destructive of our own souls as people of faith created to live in justice-seeking community with the rest of God's good creation.

The first step that first-world Christians need to take before they can begin to build relationships of solidarity across lines of social difference is to acknowledge and evaluate the ways in which privilege functions in their lives. This is enormously difficult in the context of the United States, where rhetoric about difference is often structured in antagonistic ways. Instead of recognizing differences as avenues for epistemological insights about the nature of humanity, differences become ways of separating oneself from other people and reifying the characteristics that mark personal identity as normative, or normal, which then translates into good and right. We create situations of conflict: Mexico vs. the United States, black vs. white, women vs. men, gay/lesbian/bisexual/transgender vs. straight, poor vs. rich, blue collar vs. white collar. Pitting the marginalized against the marginalizer often has the effect of shutting down debate, of laying blame, and of evoking guilt, hostility, and anger. This sort of strategy does not move toward a deeper understanding of the multiplicity of human differences that are part of God's good creation.

The point of plumbing the depths of privilege is not to elicit guilt on the part of those either perpetrating or benefiting from it. The point is for people to be honest with themselves about the ways in which social privileges are often associated with skin color, clothing and speech patterns, authority and power, age, size, ability, and sexual orientation. In order for this to happen, it is necessary to examine and understand the differences that alienate people from one another. When people are able to see their social reality with new eyes, with the eyes of other people who do not inhabit their social location and who see reality from a very different vantage point, it opens the door for empathy and for the possibility of engaging the other on the basis of mutuality. Privilege will only become visible when people recognize it as an advantage that others do not have. Only after people have opened their eyes to seeing the social relations in our world from new and different perspectives can we begin to inquire into the moral accountability of a system of economic globalization that benefits the few at the expense of the many.

Considering Privilege and Injustice in Ancient Israel

Recognition of the relationship between privilege and injustice is not only a contemporary concern; it is a prominent aspect of how social justice is addressed in the Bible. The book of Nehemiah narrates events that transpired after the southern kingdom fell to the Babylonian Empire in 586 BCE. The conquerors followed an imperial strategy of dispersion and assimilation by sending everyone but the farmers into exile in Babylon.[44] With the urban center of Jerusalem decimated, the area necessarily transitioned to an agricultural and more rural lifestyle as the farmers maintained the productive value of the land and likely supported the Babylonian Empire economically through taxation.[45]

Meanwhile, given the fact that the conquerors had relocated the most skilled and elite members of the Jewish community to Babylon, many of the exiles successfully integrated into Babylonian culture. This successful integration continued after the Babylonian Empire was conquered by the Persian Empire. Some, like Nehemiah, even found positions of power and influence within the king's court. As the cupbearer to the king, Nehemiah was a trusted servant of the Persian Empire. After Cyrus's edict opened up the possibility of the return to Judah for the exiled Jewish community, King Artaxerxes commissioned Nehemiah to return to Jerusalem as its governor. One of his first priorities was to rebuild the city wall.

The work of rebuilding the wall was not only laborious, but the threat of disruption from the leaders of the surrounding areas led to a situation of intensified work conditions. These included round-the-clock armed guards watching over the construction as well as a curfew requiring inhabitants of the city to stay within the walls until the defenses were secured. While the people were likely supportive of the efforts at rebuilding and fortification, the increased intensity of the work requirements of the able-bodied males as well as the termination of the free movement of the city dwellers seems to have caused particular unrest among the general population who bore the economic brunt of such restrictive living conditions.

The people who cried out were the working poor of the community, whose cries rose up in response to the injustice of starvation and usury that resulted from the building campaign itself. While the exact circumstances that led to this outcry are not known, it is possible to imagine the normal circumstances of a debt coming due during a time of lost income or an increase in the price of grain in a city cut off from trade with its neighbors. For the people who are required to live day-to-day, it is necessary to leave the city walls to tend their land and animals and to engage in activities of trade with the surrounding communities. If the most able-bodied workers are tied up in construction, even for a short time, the daily needs of the households cannot be met. Indeed, as the most marginalized members of the community found themselves being forced into mortgaging their farms and their houses or selling their sons and daughters into indentured servitude, the wives and mothers of the community, in particular, cried out against their Jewish kin who were taking advantage of their desperation to turn a profit through a well-placed loan or the cheap purchase of the labor of their neighbors' daughters and sons.

It is remarkable that Nehemiah, who later becomes the champion of justice, is initially one of the perpetrators of injustice. The very fact that Nehemiah, who is portrayed as a noble and venerable prophet and governor, engages in this behavior prior to the people's outcry indicates that he saw nothing wrong with the practice of lending with interest. From his perspective as a member of the wealthy elite, it appears that this practice made good business sense as well as contributing to his personal wealth and well-being. It is only when he listens to the cry of injustice and begins to look at how this behavior is impacting the lives and well-being of his fellow citizens that he begins to understand the internal damage that this behavior is doing to the life of the community at large.

For first-world citizens who live in the current economic and political centers of power in our contemporary world, Nehemiah's actions are instructive. It is often hard for people with privilege to see the ways in which their behavior—and business practices in particular—affect other people. One of the most important things that Nehemiah does is to *listen* to the people's grievances. In examining injustices perpetrated by imperial powers throughout history, one of the recurring themes is the disempowerment and disregard of the perspectives and experiences of the poor and exploited people in society.

An ethic of solidarity is built upon relationships of mutuality, which, in turn, can only develop as people build relationships of trust. Nehemiah's actions embody the description of a good leader put forth in Psalm 72:12, "He delivers the needy when they call, the poor and those who have no helper." Good leaders, be they in the political, economic or social realms of society, must always remember to pay attention to who is at the table when decisions are being made. They must ensure the broadest participation of people, including those most often overlooked in our society.

Transforming Privilege

Barbara Padilla is a Roman Catholic laywoman whose experience of *metanoia* reshaped her life in ways that led her into developing relationships of solidarity. She was marginally involved with her local parish in Tucson until 2002, when she joined a local immersion trip to Altar, Mexico. Barbara was not particularly moved by the formal presentation of the harsh realities of migrant life on the border, and her response of, "Oh, that's sad," indicates that the compassion that she felt did not translate into anything more meaningful than pity.

That is, until the group met with some migrants at a restaurant. Barbara noticed a woman sitting by herself in the corner who was about her age and who looked very sad. Wanting to talk with her, she asked a member of her group to interpret. As they talked, Barbara discovered that the woman had migrated north from Chiapas, one of the southernmost states in Mexico, in search of a better life for her children. Despite the fact that what motivated her to migrate was her children, she had left all four of them behind under her sister's care because she was uncertain about what prospects she would find after reaching the United States. As they talked, the Mexican woman began to cry and Barbara reached out to her unable to stop her own tears from flowing. As Barbara described it,

> For me, that was the moment, the feeling of knowing that *this* is the reason why I came. To see this lady and know that someone would leave their kids like that to try to make something better. That's just not right. And where was I before? Why wasn't I paying attention? Until you see people and meet people and hear the things that people go through, you just don't get it. At least I didn't.[46]

Like Barbara, many who live in the first world are familiar with the desperate conditions of poverty that drive immigrants from Mexico to seek work in the United States. The problems of child labor, human trafficking and forced prostitution, sweatshops, climate change, and a litany of the human-created social injustice in our world fill newspapers, TV broadcasts, and the Internet on a daily basis. The twenty-first-century world exhibits both dizzying wealth and extreme poverty. In 2003, 7.7 million people were millionaires.[47] Their combined wealth was $28.9 trillion US, close to three times the US GDP.[48] On the other end of the spectrum, three billion people (nearly half of the world's population) live in poverty. Every day, approximately seventy thousand children die from hunger and preventable hunger-related disease. In citing statistics on maternal mortality, the World Health Organization offers the following comparison: "[Imagine that] every four hours, day-in and day-out, a jumbo jet crashes and all on board are killed. The 250 passengers are all women, most in the prime of life, some still in their teens. . . . In India more women die in one month than in America, Europe, Japan and Australia, together, in an entire year."[49]

Environmentalists warn that the planet cannot sustain a world in which everyone consumes at the level of the developed world. In a recent course on wealth and poverty, after discussing recent philanthropic gifts of Bill Gates and Warren Buffett, one student commented, "I like the idea of these mega-wealthy people giving away so much of their money because I want that much money too, and they show you can be really rich, but still be morally good. I used to feel guilty about wanting to be rich, but now I can feel good about it." This student is certainly not alone in his morally dubious desire for excessive wealth; in 2011 the ratio of CEO pay to the average worker rose to 231:1, up from 58.5:1 in 1989 and 20:1 in 1965.[50]

The economic crisis that began in 2007 is eerily reminiscent of the words of many of the Hebrew prophets, who warned their fellow Israelites about the consequences of wealth and hubris. In describing the moral failings of the Babylonian Empire that threatened to conquer Judah, Habakkuk cried out:

> "Alas for you who heap up what is not your own!"
> How long will you load yourselves with goods taken in pledge?
> Will not your own creditors suddenly rise,
> and those who make you tremble wake up?
> Then you will be booty for them.
> Because you have plundered many nations,
> all that survive of the peoples shall plunder you—
> because of human bloodshed, and violence to the earth,
> to cities and all who live in them. (Hab. 2:6–8)

In a country where the federal deficit has exceeded $1 trillion for the past four years,[51] the ratio of household debt to disposable personal income has increased at alarming rates, peaking at 130 percent in 2007 (it had dropped to 118 percent by 2010),[52] and average student debt now exceeds $26,000 (a 40 percent increase over the past seven years),[53] Habakkuk's words are disturbingly relevant. How long can rich nations continue to promote a consumer economy and a consumer culture in which people "load [ourselves] with goods taken in pledge"? There are many nations and peoples around the world who view the United States much like the Israelites viewed the Babylonians—as a greedy empire that has plundered many nations. A recent statement adopted by the World Alliance of Reformed Churches known as the "Accra Confession" states, "The policy of unlimited growth among industrialized countries and the drive for profit of transnational corporations have plundered the earth and severely damaged the environment."[54] Even more pointedly, it goes on to say, "The government of the United States of America and its allies, together with international finance and trade institutions (International Monetary Fund, World Bank, the World Trade Organization) use political, economic, or military alliances to protect and advance the interest of capital owners."[55]

Many people of faith struggle with a multitude of difficult conversations about economics, religion, and culture as they strive to discern how they can live their lives in ways that contribute to building up the common good—a task that has become countercultural in a world bent on individualism and wealth accumulation. Perhaps the most significant moral challenge for many first-world Christians is that even after recognizing the moral failings of the present system, many people simply do not know what to do. The situation appears overwhelming—for many people, it doesn't seem possible to alter the direction of globalization. Too many people respond like Barbara did, by simply shutting down and ignoring the problem. Her question, "Why wasn't I paying attention?" is a haunting one. The guilt that can accompany recognition of complicity in a system that benefits some at the expense of others can be paralyzing.

Many twenty-first-century Christians struggle with inherited theological traditions that are inadequate for making sense of a radically plural and transnational world on the brink of ecological collapse. The challenge is to discern how to address the moral conundrum that first-world people face as they strive to live with integrity in the midst of a global economic order that has been structured to privilege individualism, wealth creation, efficiency, and the maximization of profits. In the face of negotiating the relative power and privilege that many people in the first world possess, quite frankly, "Sell what you own, and give the money to the poor" is not an adequate ethic—not simply because it is unrealistic, but more importantly because it does nothing to change the structures of our social order that are oppressive.

Barbara Padilla's experience in Mexico was a *metanoia* experience. After her encounter with the woman who was seeking a better life for her children, Barbara's worldview was transformed. She recognized that she had been reading about immigrants struggling and dying in the desert for years, but she did not know these people. Now, she knew one of them, and she decided that she was going to do whatever she could so that no mother had to endure what the woman she met was enduring. Barbara became a leader on immigrant issues in her parish and in her community. She joined Samaritans, a group that patrols the desert offering food and water to people in distress. She organized the sale of Just Coffee in her church and used the opportunity to educate people about the complex problems that prompt immigrants to leave their home countries. She began to lead parish visits to Altar that were modeled on her first trip.[56]

Barbara's experience of *metanoia* turned her life upside down as she began to live out a relationship of solidarity with the immigrants that she had met. If the first step toward transformation is for people to examine their personal and collective experiences of privilege, the second is to establish relationships of mutuality across lines of difference upon which bonds of solidarity can be built.

Notes

1. Carmen DeNavas-Walt, Bernadetta D. Proctor, and Jessica C. Smith, *Income, Poverty, and Health Insurance Coverage in the United States: 2010* (Washington, DC: US Census Bureau, September 2011), 10.

2. Recent attention to extreme poverty (defined as living under $1.25 a day) by the UN Millennium Development Goals and the World Bank has helped reduce extreme poverty from 1.94 billion people in 1981 to 1.29 billion people in 2008. Slower strides have been made in reducing the number of people living under $2 a day (the World Bank definition of "poverty," as opposed to "extreme poverty"), with the numbers falling from 2.59 billion in 1981 to 2.47 billion in 2008. "World Bank Sees Progress Against Extreme Poverty, But Flags Vulnerabilities," World Bank Press release #2012/297/DEC, February 29, 2012.

3. "What is 'wealthy'?" *USB Investor Watch*, 3Q 2013.

4. "Class Project," *New York Times* poll, question #16, March 13–14, 2005, http://www.nytimes.com/packages/html/national/20050515_CLASS_GRAPHIC/index_04.html.

5. Jared Bernstein, Lawrence Mishel, and Sylvia A. Allegretto, *State of Working America 2006/2007* (New York: Cornell University Press, 2007), 95.

6. Peggy McIntosh, "White Privilege: Unpacking the Invisible Knapsack," in *Race, Class, and Gender in the United States*, 6th ed., ed. Paula Rothenberg (New York: Worth, 2004), 191.

7. Ibid.

8. Ibid., 191.

9. Sally Matthews, "Inherited or Earned Advantage?" *Mail and Guardian*, September 12, 2011.

10. Ibid.

11. Mary Elizabeth Hobgood, *Dismantling Privilege: An Ethics of Accountability* (Cleveland: Pilgrim, 2000), 2.

12. For an excellent social analysis that illustrates this point by examining the formation of black ghettos in the United States, see David Hilfiker, *Urban Injustice: How Ghettos Happen* (New York: Seven Stories, 2002).

13. Peggy McIntosh, "White Privilege and Male Privilege: A Personal Account of Coming to See Correspondences Through Work in Women's Studies" (working paper #189, Wellesley College Center for Research on Women, Wellesley, MA, 1988).

14. Mary R. Sawyer, *The Church on the Margins: Living Christian Communities* (New York: Continuum, 2003), 43.

15. Ibid., 27.

16. "A Nation Challenged: Choice of Words; Mission Title May Change," *New York Times*, September 21, 2001, http://www.nytimes.com/2001/09/21/us/a-nation-challenged-choice-of-words-mission-title-may-change.html.

17. See George E. Tinker, *Missionary Conquest: The Gospel and Native American Cultural Genocide* (Minneapolis: Fortress Press, 1993), for a detailed analysis of the interplay between religion, economics, and colonialism.

18. Sawyer, *Church on the Margins*, 23.

19. Ibid., 24.

20. Katie Cannon, "Slave Ideology and Biblical Interpretation," in *Katie's Canon: Womanism and the Soul of the Black Community* (New York: Continuum, 1995), 39.

21. Ibid., 40.

22. David Brion Davis, *Inhuman Bondage: The Rise and Fall of Slavery in the New World* (New York: Oxford, 2006), 66–67.

23. Ibid., 64–73

24. Ibid., 187.

25. Cannon, "Slave Ideology and Biblical Tradition," 40.

26. Davis, *Inhuman Bondage*, 187.

27. Ralph Eubanks, interview with Rebecca Roberts, *Talk of the Nation*, National Public Radio, January 18, 2010.

28. Michelle Alexander, *The New Jim Crow: Mass Incarceration in an Age of Colorblindness* (New York: The New Press, 2010).

29. Emilie M. Townes, "From Mammy to Welfare Queen: Images of Black Women in Public Policy Formation," in *Beyond Slavery: Overcoming Its Religious and Sexual Legacies*, ed. Bernadette J. Brooten (New York: Palgrave, 2010), 61–74.

30. Hilfiker, *Urban Injustice,* 21–22.

31. Ibid., 4.

32. Ibid., 6.

33. Ibid., 7.

34. Ibid., 6.

35. Miguel de la Torre, "For Immigrants," in *To Do Justice: A Guide for Progressive Christians* ed. Rebecca Todd Peters and Elizabeth Hinson-Hasty (Louisville: Westminster John Knox, 2008), 74–75.

36. Joseph Barndt, *Understanding and Dismantling Racism: The Twenty-First Century Challenge to White America* (Minneapolis: Fortress Press, 2007), 35.

37. "US Census Bureau Economic Indicators," http://www.census.gov/cgi-bin/briefroom/BriefRm.

38. Centers for Disease Control and Prevention, *National Vital Statistics Report* 59, no. 4 (2011): 6.

39. US Census Bureau, "Table 720. Family Net Worth—Mean and Median Net Worth in Constant (2007) Dollars by Selected Family Characteristics: 1998–2007," in *Statistical Abstract of the United States: 2011*, http://www.census.gov/prod/2011pubs/11statab/income.pdf. It is important to note that net worth measures assets minus debt, which is not the same as income.

40. Paul Taylor, Richard Fry, and Rakesh Kochar, "Wealth Gaps Rise to Record Highs Between Whites, Blacks, Hispanics," in *Social and Demographic Trends* (Washington, DC: Pew Research Center, July 26, 2011), http://pewsocialtrends.org/files/2011/07/SDT-Wealth-Report_7-26-11_FINAL.pdf, p.1.

41. Nicolas D. Kristof, "Racism Without Racists," *New York Times*, October 4, 2008, http://www.nytimes.com/2008/10/05/opinion/05kristof.html?_r=0.

42. Ibid.

43. Ibid.

44. Jacob M. Myers, *Ezra-Nehemiah,* Anchor Yale Bible Commentaries (New Haven: Yale University Press, 1995), xx.

45. Jon L. Berquist, "Resistance and Accommodation in the Roman Empire," in *In The Shadow of the Empire: Reclaiming the Bible as a History of Faithful Resistance,* ed. Richard A. Horsley (Louisville: Westminster John Knox, 2008), 42.

46. Jeffry Odell Korgen, *Solidarity Will Transform the World: Stories of Hope from Catholic Relief Services* (Maryknoll, NY: Orbis, 2007), 28.

47. Commission for Justice, Peace and Creation, "Alternative Globalization Addressing People and the Earth—AGAPE document," (World Council of Churches, 2006), 3.

48. Ibid.

49. World Health Organization, "Maternal mortality: helping women off the road to death," *WHO Chronicle* 40, no. 5 (1986): 175–83.

50. This data is based on averaging specific firm CEO-to-worker compensation ratios rather than averages of CEO and worker compensation. The 2011 ratios are down from their peak of 383:1 in 2000. Lawrence Mishel, Josh Bivens, Elise Gould, and Heidi Shierholz, *State of Working America*, 12th edition (Ithaca: Cornell University Press, 2012), 285.

51. The US Federal budget deficit peaked in 2009 at .4 trillion and fell to just under trillion in 2012. It is projected to fall even further in 2013. White House Office of Management and Budget, *Historical Tables: Table 1.1—Summary of Receipts, Outlays, and Surpluses or Deficits: 1789–2018*.

52. Reuven Glick and Kevin J. Lansing, "Consumers and the Economy, Part I: Household Credit and Personal Saving," *FRBSF (Federal Reserve Bank San Francisco) Economic Letter*, January 10, 2011. See Katherine Porter, ed., *Broke: How Debt Bankrupts the Middle Class* (Stanford: Stanford University Press, 2012) for an excellent social analysis of the problem of debt and bankruptcy for the middle class in the United States.

53. Joseph E. Stiglitz, "Student Debt and the Crushing of the American Dream," *New York Times*, Opinionator, May 12, 2013.

54. "Covenanting for Justice in the Economy and the Earth (Accra Confession)," (World Alliance of Reformed Churches, Accra, Ghana, 2004), paragraph 8.

55. Ibid., paragraph 13.

56. Korgen, *Solidarity*, 27–29.

5

Embodying Solidarity, Living into Justice

Trying to figure out what solidarity with the two-thirds world looks like is a difficult topic for people who live in the first world. One reason for this is that they undoubtedly benefit from the current model of economic globalization that dominates our world. Most middle-class people own stocks, mutual funds, bonds, or IRAs. While stock portfolios may have taken a hit in the recent recession, many people profited from the booming bull market of the 1990s. Many people check the daily stock reports or their quarterly statements with excited anticipation as they watch their retirement accounts grow. But morally responsible Christians must ask, Whose backs are bearing the burden of these growing mutual funds? Whose eyes or fingers are being destroyed in the manufacture of the clothing in our closets and electronic equipment in our homes? And what will the world be like for our children and our children's children?

Like the Israelites, we do not always pay attention to God, particularly when God challenges the comfortableness of our lives. We sit in the air-conditioned comfort of our homes, well fed, mostly satisfied or at least entertained by our possessions, and it is easy to believe that God rejoices with us in our success. After all, doesn't God want what is best for us? It seems to me that the answer is both yes and no. Of course God rejoices in our success and wants us to be healthy, well fed, and happy, but this cannot come at the expense of the livelihood of the rest of the earth community. It cannot come at the expense of the burning of Thai workers or the blinding of Mexican maquiladora workers or the labor of Indian children. Of course, it is much easier to think and talk about being in solidarity with those at the opposite end of the economic spectrum than it is to figure out how to really live a life of solidarity that is meaningful and authentic. In this final chapter, I will offer three concrete strategies that people can employ to begin to embody an ethic of solidarity in their daily lives.

Living into Justice

Every day we are forced to make dozens of moral decisions that impact the health and well-being of our neighbors, many of whom we do not know and *can never know*. This is true when people make decisions as consumers about whether to purchase locally produced organic food rather than conventional products shipped in from Chile, Argentina, or even California, when people choose to use cloth diapers rather than disposable, to buy clothes in resale shops rather from retailers, or when they decide to bike to work or take public transportation rather than driving a car. Each day, we are called upon to make seemingly insignificant decisions that are, in fact, morally significant. All of our decisions are important because they can build up our local economies, reduce our environmental footprint, and contribute to our own health and well-being in the process, or they can build up the profit margins of corporations and their stockholders, create more waste and pollution, and contribute to the increasing economic and social divisions in our world.

Once we are able to move to a position of mutuality as the starting point for our moral reflection, we are able to exercise our moral agency in ways that reflect an understanding of the deep interdependence of our lives with the lives of all peoples and creatures on the earth. From this new worldview, we are able to acknowledge that every action we take toward living our lives in more sustainable and justice-oriented ways is morally significant. Most of our actions are simply a reflection of habits that we have developed, rather than conscious choices we make. What we eat, the clothes we wear, where we shop, bank, and socialize are often habitual actions of everyday life. We become so accustomed to our habits and routines that we often forget about the larger implications of our choices and decisions. If we desire to live out an ethic of solidarity, we must think about the implications of our actions and live more intentionally in the world.

Clearly, it is important to take an inventory of all the areas of our lives and examine ways in which we can change our habits and behavior to decrease both our environmental impact and our exploitation of workers in the developing world. As we engage in this inventory, we will need to look at least at the areas of transportation, food, clothing, money, housing, recreation/entertainment, and energy. Each of these areas represents significant financial power on our part as well as significant strains on our environment.

In our consumer-oriented global economy, one instrument of power that each of us possess is our money. Consumer demand has the power to shift global trade practices, and we, as consumers, can participate in changing the direction of the global economy by exercising our purchasing power in morally responsible ways. Let me be clear: I am NOT saying that shopping is patriotic, nor do I mean to give the impression that you should go shopping to be in solidarity with the world's poor! There are certainly some people who argue that the best thing US Americans can do for the economy and for the poor in developing countries is to shop, to spend our money, because increased consumer demand increases global trade and consequently increases jobs, at home and abroad.

My argument is a little more complex. It is true that our purchasing power can be an important resource for marshaling moral changes in our economic activity, but what I am suggesting is not that we increase our spending so much as that we are more intentional about how we make the purchases that are necessary for our survival. We do not live in a subsistence economy, where everyone is able to provide for their own needs and the needs of their families, and I do not think that in order for us to build a sustainable world we need to move back to primarily subsistence patterns of living. We live in a world and a society in which we must purchase many of the basic essentials for life. You might begin by asking, "What are the ways in which the money that I allocate out of my budget to spend on food, clothing, and shelter can be spent to reduce my environmental impact and increase my solidarity with people in the two-thirds world?"

Given our present economy, it will not always be possible to make choices that allow us to use our money in socially responsible ways. We can, however, take advantage of the opportunities that we currently do have (buying fair trade products, buying local and organic produce and meats, and being more intentional about supporting clothing companies that enforce fair trade practices). This may very well mean that some aspects of our life may change.

For instance, our eating habits may change. We know that domestically raised factory-farmed meat is cheaper because the production process exploits the environment and the animals and because the federal government subsidizes the feed. Imported meat products are also often cheaper for a variety of reasons, but their environmental impact can be quite high. It might surprise you to know that the global production of livestock contributes 18 percent of total greenhouse gas emissions, which is an even higher percentage than the transportation sector.[1] Currently, one-third of Earth's land surface is being used for livestock production, including 70 percent of the former forests in the Amazon.[2] When many people see the prices for locally raised, organic and biodynamic meat, they often complain that it is too expensive. The question, though, is, "Too expensive for what?" Perhaps it is too expensive for everyday purchase, but if it reflects the actual production cost of such a product, perhaps reducing our consumption of meat is part of what it means to live in solidarity with the one-third of the world's people who live in absolute poverty.

Furthermore, in much of our consumer interactions we should be asking, Why is this product so cheap? Is it poorly made? Did its production contribute to increased greenhouse gases, or deforestation, or the exploitation of farm workers? For people living in poverty and for many people in the working class, shopping at Walmart and other big-box discount retailers is an economic necessity that requires serious public conversations about living wages; adequate public transportation; high-quality, affordable child care; and adequate health care.[3] However, many people in the middle and upper-middle class have simply been trained to look for "bargains," to buy the cheapest products available, and to demand "discounted" prices. Advertising campaigns that highlight Walmart's "always low prices" or Kmart's "blue light specials" both cater to and reinforce US consumer attitudes about cheap prices.

Using our purchasing power strategically is one way that consumers can gain some measure of control over the ways in which they interact with the global economy. Socially responsible investing (SRI) is one example of how financial power can be exercised to make a difference. SRI is a contemporary movement that focuses on applying values to investment decisions. But in a way it is nothing new; church bodies have a rich history of refusing to do business with those who profited from slavery, weapons, or war. During the twentieth century, avoiding companies that profited from the production of alcohol, tobacco, and gambling became the earliest example of a socially responsible "sin" screen used for mutual fund investments. And many churches and denominations were deeply involved with the divestment of corporations from South Africa that led to the downfall of the apartheid regime. Today, many denominations, congregations, and religious organizations support the Interfaith Center for Corporate Responsibility (ICCR), which has been a leading sponsor of social proposals at annual stockholder meetings for the past thirty years. Being socially responsible with our finances is something that each of us can get involved with at the household level and with our church budgets and financial resources. Screening stock portfolios (both personal retirement funds and church assets) by a list of socially responsible values that complement your values or the mission of your church is one of the primary ways that individuals and churches can get involved with socially responsible investing. Many denominations have established sets of screens that can be used for this purpose.

A second area of SRI is shareholder advocacy. Even after employing the traditional "sin" screen for companies involved with weapons, war, alcohol, and tobacco, there remain a number of companies whose practices regarding labor, environmental, and social impact could be improved. The ICCR works on behalf of 275 communities of faith across the country to raise issues of social justice and to hold transnational corporations accountable to their stockholders. While most of the shareholder resolutions do not have the votes necessary to pass, they succeed in bringing important issues and problems into public view, and the corporations subsequently address many of these issues. In 1999, two years of activist organizing culminated in a shareholder resolution asking Home Depot to stop the sale of old-growth wood products in their stores. While the resolution was defeated, shortly after the annual meeting Home Depot announced the phasing out of wood products from environmentally sensitive areas. Within months, Lowe's and other do-it-yourself chains followed suit. Big-box retailers hold an enormous amount of economic power based on their annual revenue and purchasing scale. Shifts of scale like these can have an important impact on environmental and labor rights issues in our global economy.

A third area of SRI is community investing in the form of supporting community banks and micro-credit lending. Generally speaking, community investing encourages people to invest money in their local communities rather than work with multinational financial institutions that often use their deposits to promote development in growing markets across the country or even overseas. Because community banks are locally owned and their mission is to support the development of their communities, they are often able to provide more individual assessment of risk than impersonal scoring systems that focus solely on statistics and financial history. Loan officers at these institutions are empowered to make decisions based on the merits of business plans and the character of loan applicants in ways that larger banks simply cannot. Community banks offer services that are competitive with the larger banks; by switching your personal and church's financial assets to a community bank, you can contribute to the development of your local community in important ways.

Micro-credit is another form of community investing, in which small sums of money are loaned to people who want to start small businesses but need some initial capital investment in order to begin. Professor Muhammad Yunus of Bangladesh received a Nobel Peace Prize in 2006 for his pioneering work with micro-credit through the Grameen Bank. Oikocredit is one of the largest community investment vehicles in the world and was originally founded by religious organizations, including the World Council of Churches. Community notes pay what is known as a "philanthropic interest rate" (usually 2 percent), and church reserves that often sit in bank accounts as backup for emergencies could instead be used to help people in poverty gain a new lease on life.

One example of how micro-credit works is the Sinapi Aba Trust in Ghana, West Africa. A group of Christian churches formed this trust in 1994 as a nongovernmental organization with the purpose of offering small loans to local entrepreneurs. They adopted the name "Sinapi Aba," or "mustard seed" in the local language, in recognition of the parable of the mustard seed where the smallest seed can bear great fruit. The small loans (or micro-loans) are offered to women like Alice Amoateng, who dreamed of starting a small business trading clothes.[4] Though Alice's husband is a teacher with a regular income, the family could not support themselves on his salary alone. When she heard about Sinapi Aba, she applied for and received a loan to start her business. Because most of the women lack collateral, the trust bank works through a system of community accountability in which a group of loan recipients agree to secure the loans of others in their group if one of them fails to repay.

Not surprisingly, the micro-credit model has found that investing in the training and leadership development of poor and low-income women around the world is having more than just an economic benefit for the women's immediate families. Alice's leadership training gave her the confidence she needed to run for the District Assembly. Now, thanks to her initiative, the primary school in her village has been renovated, she organizes regular community work to keep her village clean, and she is seeking funds to improve the roads in her community. Sharing our resources with women, children, and families across the globe may mean a lower interest rate for our own savings plans, but it may also mean the difference between life and death for the people it helps. Imagine the number of people your retirement savings or your church's reserve funds could be helping given the fact that Alice's loan and most micro-credit loans range from fifty to one hundred dollars! Sinapi Aba is just one example of hundreds of community micro-credit programs that are helping improve the lives of poor people around the world, and building up civil society and the health of communities in the process. Micro-credit offers us another concrete example of how we can shift our habits and practices in ways that promote solidarity with our global neighbors.

Changing our habits and practices is important on at least two levels. First, we are talking about an area of life over which we have some measure of control: our money and our time and how we choose to spend them. It can be enormously satisfying to restructure our daily routines in ways that allow us to live out our values by choosing to walk to work, hang our clothes out to dry, shop at a local farmer's market, use a local bank, or eat at a locally owned restaurant. Each of these choices can collectively contribute to a real shift in our own way of being in the world. This sort of immediate gratification is important for helping us keep up our morale as we struggle against a status quo that threatens to overwhelm us.

Second, while we may begin to make these changes as we act out of a moral intuition of responsibility, each little shift in our behavior contributes to a larger shift in our consciousness, leading us deeper and deeper into the experience of *metanoia* until we get to the point where we really do see the world in a new way. Once our worldview shifts to incorporate a new understanding of our relationship with our brothers and sisters who are living in poverty, and our actions produce changes in our own lifestyles that reflect our new awareness, we are beginning to live out an ethic of solidarity. While it is imperative to change the way that we live on an individual level, an ethic of solidarity requires that our analysis and our action move beyond this to the level of social analysis. As we think about the ways in which people of faith can respond to poverty and environmental degradation in our world, the second strategy that I would like to consider is reshaping the economic structures of society.

Solidarity Economics

An ethic of solidarity offers a moral foundation for building a new set of economic, political, and social relations that respond to the very real needs of a planet in crisis and a human community where half of the population lives in poverty. When solidarity is understood as the voluntary action of individuals and groups working together across lines of difference toward a common good, it represents a different paradigm for human behavior and relationships than either individualism or collectivism, the moral foundations of capitalism and communism.

A moral norm of solidarity as the foundation for economic policy and exchange begins with two key theological principles as its starting point: the sacredness of life and the interdependence of the human community and the natural world. If economic policy were to begin from these starting points, it would be much more difficult to create labor and environmental policies that exploited or harmed people and the environment. Furthermore, these theological principles would also translate into economic policy that had a different set of assumptions about the nature of both economics and markets than the assumptions that guide free-market capitalism. The following three assumptions would certainly create a different landscape for the development of economic policy:

1) Economics and markets are public tools that are used to shape society in particular ways.
2) Economic and social policies are integrally related and must reflect attention to both individuals and the common good.
3) The primary purpose of a solidarity economy is to increase the general well-being of humanity and the Earth.[5]

The solidarity economy represents a radically new foundation for political, economic, and social arrangements as a human community. Ultimately, a solidarity economy would be built on a different social narrative than the cultural myths of "rugged individualism" and self-sufficiency that shape the contemporary US political economy in ways that lay the burden of responsibility for success solely on the backs of individuals. This does not mean that a norm of solidarity absolves individuals from being *responsible*, but it recognizes that the human condition of interdependence requires the development of structures in society within which people are able to function responsibly. Creating stable social networks in society that provide for the development of thriving communities is an achievable goal. A solidarity economy must be built on a social narrative of community, compassion, and a radical mutuality that recognizes and affirms the interdependence of human life and the natural world. An ethic of solidarity offers creative ways of shaping economic behavior as a human community rooted in the Christian ethical principles of social justice and sustainability.

Within the context of a global free-market economy, it is difficult to imagine what an alternative economy might look like. Nevertheless, even within the dominance of neoliberalism, there are vibrant examples of businesses, communities, and workers who are organizing their economic life in ways that embrace sustainability and social justice and challenge the dominant assumptions of the neoliberalism and free-market capitalism. From fair trade practices to worker co-ops, from community-supported agriculture to local currencies, people in the United States and around the world are struggling to set up alternative economic structures (e.g. businesses, currencies, markets) that embody the values of a solidarity economy.

The word *economy* comes from the Greek words *oikos,* meaning "household," and *nomos,* meaning "law" or "management."[6] While we commonly associate the idea of economic systems with monetary economies, the reality is that economies are human ways to order the exchange of goods and services in our cultures. As the Greek roots indicate, they are how we manage our households. Not all economic systems require money. There are a variety of economic systems that have existed and continue to exist to order human economic transactions. In fact, most people engage in a variety of forms of economic activity on a daily basis, and most people employ a wide variety of values as they make decisions about providing for their families and engaging in economic exchange. On a practical level, we recognize the value of trading, collectivism, altruism, reciprocity, and sharing as essential and productive aspects of our economic life. Unfortunately, since we have not been taught to think about these actions as part of mainstream economics, we do not fully appreciate their economic value and the potential that alternative economic models offer for addressing the social crises that we face as a human community.

For instance, in extended networks of families and friends, people are engaged in a gift economy—meaning that people do things for one another without expecting anything in return. When friends invite one another over for dinner or offer to watch each other's children, they are exchanging goods and services, but they are operating within a framework of friendship and family that reflects deep moral bonds of love, compassion, and a genuine concern for one another's well-being. There is no expectation of *quid pro quo,* where people keep track of one another's actions and expect a corresponding deed in return. The kind of reciprocity that relationships like this model is an altruistic behavior that is rooted in what economist Nancy Folbre has termed "the invisible heart." This is in marked contrast to Adam Smith's concept of "the invisible hand" that he described as guiding the behavior of markets.[7] Folbre's term is intended to demonstrate that many daily interpersonal actions and transactions are motivated by care and compassion rather than the self-interest that modern economists claim as the motivation for human behavior.

Another example of an alternative economy are the religious communities in which individuals and families contribute money in the form of tithes and offerings toward the collective goal of running a church and contributing to the well-being of a community. When people pool their resources, they are able to hire pastors, musicians, secretaries, janitors, day care workers, and other personnel to work with a congregation toward achieving the common goals of their mission and ministry. Churches, synagogues, mosques and other religious communities provide many services, including fellowship, spiritual guidance, counseling, child care, youth activities, opportunities for community activism and volunteerism, worship, prayer, and countless other tangible and intangible benefits. No one, however, is *charged* for these services. Even more significantly, people are not asked how much they contributed when they come in the door of a religious institution; the services provided are shared freely with all members of the community who are interested. In most religious communities, tithing is voluntary and anonymous. Faith communities and the ways that they organize themselves socially and economically represent collective economics, where a group of people organize their relationships and economic affairs in a way that stresses the collective or common good over individual needs and desires.

In barter economies, goods and services are exchanged without any money needing to change hands. A new social movement known as "time banking" is a contemporary barter economy model in which people trade goods or services with others in their community. For instance, if someone provides an hour of English language tutoring, they might later redeem an hour of babysitting from someone else in the network. Time banks make a number of socially valuable contributions to local economies and communities. They promote community building by encouraging citizens to get to know their neighbors in new ways through reciprocal relationships of trust that build up around the exchange of things like child care, running errands, household projects, and tutoring. They can also increase community respect and individual self-worth by encouraging community members to identify their own assets and talents and valuing these as meaningful contributions to society. When a variety of previously devalued tasks or activities like tutoring, chauffeuring, or grocery shopping are recognized as valuable contributions to the functioning of a local community, it can help people to rethink preconceived ideas about the value and definition of "work" as well the meaning of "community." More than eighty-five time banks in the United States are registered with TimeBanks USA, a nonprofit dedicated to supporting and promoting the time banking movement.[8]

In addition to these examples of nonmonetary economies, solidarity economies also have room for monetary exchanges, and profits are still an essential aspect to be considered. However, within a solidarity economy, maximizing profits is not the only consideration. Workers, the environment, and the local community are all recognized as stakeholders that contribute to the health and vitality of any business enterprise, and none of these are comprised in pursuit of wealth. Creativity, ingenuity, and entrepreneurial instincts are central to the task of imagining alternative economic strategies that uphold the values of a solidarity economy. One strategy is to emphasize worker democracy by establishing a cooperative business in which all workers have a say in what to do with the financial profits. In some cases the profits (or a portion of them) are reinvested in the business itself to help with routine maintenance, to grow capacity, to increase publicity, or for any number of other strategic investments to ensure the health and vitality of the business. In other cases, a portion of the profits might be set aside as a social capital fund that workers can access to help improve the quality of their lives.

This type of arrangement is a common practice with the organization TransFair USA, which runs an intensive fair trade certification program. In order to receive the TransFair certification label, participating businesses must deposit 12 percent of retail sales into a fund governed by a workers' committee to be used to invest in the social development of the workers and their families. In Ecuador, flower farmers have used these "social premium" funds for computer training classes for workers and their children, for small loans to help workers build homes, to hire a company dentist, to start an English-language program for children, and to start a hot water program for the community.[9] These programs not only provided significant material improvements in the lives of the workers, but they were also part of a larger business philosophy in which the workers are treated with dignity and respect and paid wages and benefits that have significantly improved the quality of their lives. Worker cooperatives provide over 100 million jobs internationally, which is 20 percent more than multinational corporations.[10]

These cooperatives exist in developed countries as well, with Mondragon as the most highly touted example. Over the past fifty years, the community of Mondragon in the Basque region of Spain has built a network of over 250 cooperative businesses that employs over eighty thousand workers. With profits of 1.78 million euros, it is the eleventh-largest business in Spain.[11]

Worker co-ops, however, are not the only possibility for organizing business enterprises in a solidarity economy. Economist David Korten has commented that the deep changes that are needed in our economic system cannot come from individual responsible businesses: "They require building a new economy comprised of responsible, locally-rooted businesses that function within a framework of community values and accountability."[12] The Business Alliance for Local Living Economies (BALLE) is a network of locally owned, socially responsible businesses that are working together to support one another and to build vibrant local communities. BALLE is made up of over eighty community networks in the United States and Canada that represent over twenty-two thousand small, local businesses.[13] The principles that guide their work include a commitment to sharing prosperity, which they accomplish by seeking to "provide meaningful living wage jobs, create opportunities for broad-based business ownership, engage in fair trade, and expect living returns from our capital."[14]

The global economic crisis that began in 2007 represents a failure of society to recognize that the reigning economic model is not a value-free system, but one laden with values that favor profit and economic gain over other priorities such as sustainability and economic justice. Economic activity and the theory that undergirds it is a human creation that is intended to serve the needs of human societies. As a reflection of the actions of the human community in attending to the necessity of trade and economic transactions for human survival, economic activity is inherently an expression of moral behavior precisely because it is human behavior. Since economic systems are human constructions, they can be constructed in ways that reflect and respect the values of human communities. A new economic model is needed that self-consciously understands the ways in which values are embedded in political economy. Such an economic model would not focus on growth and trade as the primary indicators of success, but on the health and well-being of workers and the environment, the reduction of infant mortality, starvation relief, healthcare delivery, the feeding of the most impoverished people, and the control of HIV/AIDS for all people, rich and poor. This new economic model need not eschew profit, or growth, or efficiency, but it should recognize the ways in which it values these goals. Furthermore, it must balance them with other moral considerations, such as sustainability, justice, and the social well-being of people and communities.

From an ethical perspective that seeks to promote justice and human well-being, the human community can no longer continue to follow a model of economic theory that does not incorporate these values into its economic rationality. Constructing a solidarity economy based on the principles of justice and sustainability is possible. Such a market system would mediate against the exploitation of workers and harm to the environment. Furthermore, the engines of a solidarity economy could function to develop new economic structures and delivery systems that promote economic stability and health in vulnerable communities and populations both domestically and internationally.

CREATING COMMUNITIES OF SOLIDARITY

Changes in personal habits and lifestyle choices are essential as US Americans work to reduce our environmental footprint to a more sustainable level. At the same time, we all recognize the futility of changing our individual behavior if we do not simultaneously work to change social structures that contribute to injustice and exploitation. The steps that I have identified thus far will help to contribute to the possibility of changing the direction of globalization in our world.

However, if we truly hope to move into an ethic of solidarity, one final step is required. An ethic of solidarity that moves beyond charity requires a realignment of our relationships. We must move beyond pity and guilt toward recognition of our common humanity and an understanding that our well-being is interdependent with all of God's created order. In order to move in this direction, we must develop relationships of solidarity with real people who are different from us. Cedar Grove United Methodist Church in North Carolina is one community of faith that has reached beyond the traditional borders of their comfort zone to develop a ministry of solidarity that is transforming their church and their community in response to challenges of racism, fear, violence, poverty, and affluence that threatened to disrupt life in their rural community. Their story is important because it stands as a witness to all of us regarding the ways in which we can begin to build relationships of solidarity in our own communities that can contribute to the experience of *metanoia* and transformation.

Cedar Grove is a small, white Methodist church in the Piedmont area of North Carolina. In 2003, when their new pastor, Grace Hackney, arrived, the congregation was rebuilding from a recent arson that destroyed the sanctuary. As Grace tells the story, she made it a regular habit of standing around outside watching the construction and chatting with local residents who stopped by to monitor the progress. She met a lot of people she might not usually have met in her role as a new pastor in this community, and she regularly invited people who were not church members to join them for worship, including local African-Americans. She also made it a practice of apologizing to African-Americans for the history of the United Methodist Church in its complicity with slavery and its segregation of black and white congregations in earlier years. Her candor and approachability were noticeable in the community and made Grace and her church more accessible to the local residents.

About a year into her ministry, she received a visit from Valee Taylor, a local African-American man who had come to seek her assistance in responding to the murder of a local storeowner, Bill King. Before Bill and his wife Emma had bought the little grocery, it had been a hangout for local crack dealers. The Kings had cleaned up the store, asked the dealers to leave, and established their store as a local community gathering place. In this small farming community where everyone knew each other, Bill often allowed people to purchase groceries on credit. Some locals suspected that his murder was racially motivated, as Bill was white and Emma is black. The local black community was frustrated with the lack of response to this crime by the sheriff's department, and Valee had come to ask Grace if Cedar Grove UMC would be willing to put up some money for a reward to help catch the culprit. Here are Grace's words about what happened next:

> So, I had some church folks with me when he stopped by and we sat down and thought of what would be a good response. And the Christian response was to not let fear dominate us because that little store was a place where people gathered and people were now afraid to go there. And I said we are not a people who are dominated by fear and so we should not be afraid to go to that store. And so we decided that instead of raising money to try and find the killer, that we would have a prayer vigil at the store and invite the community to come as a sign of solidarity and peacemaking and by doing that the killer might see that witness. And so we did that and it was amazing. Over one hundred people showed up and we had no clue what was going to happen.[15]

Valee described that prayer vigil as a mystical experience: "The sunlight was shining down on us, the air was crisp, there was a light breeze. Here were blacks and whites together praying for peace in the community."[16] Valee's mother, Scenobia Taylor, a fifth-generation descendant of sharecroppers and daughter of the county's richest landowner, was also at that vigil. After the murder, she had a vision that she was to give five acres of land to someone who would use it for reconciliation. At the vigil, it became apparent to Scenobia that she was supposed to give this land to Cedar Grove United Methodist Church.

Grace had been working with her church to discuss issues of social justice since her arrival over a year before the murder and the prayer vigil. They had been discussing what gifts they had as a community, and they had been studying John Wesley and how he worked with and for the poor. While Cedar Grove UMC is a middle-class church, within a five-mile radius there are at least twenty families without indoor plumbing.[17] In their discussions, they realized that the new face of the poor in contemporary America was no longer starvation, but obesity! Poor nutritional habits and lack of access to quality fresh foods have contributed to an epidemic of obesity in our country, particularly among the poor who can often more readily afford junk food than healthier alternatives. As members of a rural farming community, they recognized that one of their main resources was land. Church members began to talk about how it was a sin for them, as a church, to live in a place where people in their own community did not have access to healthy food.

These conversations laid the groundwork for what eventually became the Anathoth Community Garden, named after the field that Jeremiah bought during the Babylonian siege (Jeremiah 32). As the community in Cedar Grove felt like it too was under siege—from drug dealers, poverty, and a shifting global economy—their action of building a community garden as a witness for peace felt like following in Jeremiah's footsteps. Scenobia's plot of land, which is less than a quarter mile from where Bill King was murdered, has been leased to the church for one dollar a year for ninety-nine years, or until she dies. It is now home to a thriving community garden where church members, local residents, and local kids serving community service hours work together growing a garden and building solidarity. In addition to the traditional black and white residents of the local community, the forces of globalization have contributed to an increasing number of Hispanic migrant farm workers in the area. Many have been forced to abandon their own farms in Central and South America because of falling commodity prices and seek work as farm laborers in the United States. As the garden project developed, many of these immigrant farmers were invited to grow food at Anathoth for their own consumption.[18]

When asked what kind of social change he sees as a result of the garden, garden manager Fred Bahnson responded,

> It's come in small doses. I guess that is how it happens everywhere. You are not going to see any radical shifts in Cedar Grove. I think that the changes I see are people interacting who wouldn't normally interact. Blacks and whites having a laugh together while they fill the garden bed. You know, people who are on opposite ends of the economic spectrum hanging out together and having a good time. People don't get that chance to interact in our society. You know, you go to the mall and buy your stuff and come home. You go to work and interact with those people and you come home. Its all these little divisions that are set up in our society and so this is a place where it's broken down and where everyone can come and interact and hopefully build friendships.[19]

In reflecting on the social problems in her community, Grace commented,

> I think that our role is not to end homelessness or to end poverty, but to create the kind of community where homelessness or poverty is not an option. So how do we create that kind of community? As Christians we have a model for how to do that. And so its not our job to break down barriers but rather it is our job to accept the grace

to be able to live as though we really do believe that those barriers don't exist. It's a fine line.[20]

The work of solidarity is never easy, and it is often met with opposition. Despite the important work that is being accomplished in the Anathoth garden, the community of Cedar Grove, North Carolina remains mired in drug-related violence. Just after Thanksgiving 2007, Grace sent out a pastoral letter to the community that detailed a recent murder and several robberies that had occurred in local stores and homes, one requiring the hospitalization of a clerk who was stabbed. Grace continues to call her church to the biblical vision of being peacemakers as she challenges them to think about how they can act together as a community of faith to respond to the recent violence, here is an excerpt from a pastoral letter she sent to the community:

> As we enter the Season of Advent, I call us to be in prayer and holy conversation about how God may be calling us as a community to respond [to these acts of violence]. What if all of the Northern Orange County churches responded with a peaceful candlelight demonstration, at the site of each of these acts of violence? What if we rented the recently evacuated Millcreek Store as a safe haven for youth to come together, as a witness to the Peace that Christ makes possible in these days of terror, learning an alternative "high" to the rush they find through the use of drugs? How is God calling us to respond?[21]

The story of Cedar Grove is a story of solidarity. In reaching out to hold the prayer vigil at King's store, at the very site of his murder, a white church reached out in friendship and solidarity to a black community living in grief and fear. By giving her land to a white church for a project of racial reconciliation, Scenobia Taylor reached out in partnership and solidarity across the traditional racial divides of a rural North Carolina community. By intentionally building the garden to include blacks, whites, and Hispanic immigrants, this ministry is daily building relationships of trust and goodwill that are the foundation for an ethic of solidarity. By risking moving out of their comfort zone and responding to problems of inequality, racism, immigration, and poverty in their community, the white, middle-class congregation of Cedar Grove United Methodist Church is actively engaged in living out an ethic of solidarity that has the capacity to change the direction of our world. The work that they are doing together is more important than the vegetables that they produce or the families that they feed. In working together, side by side, these community members are building relationships with real people that move beyond the racial and cultural stereotypes that are promoted in our society. They are building a foundation of trust upon which future acts of solidarity can be built.

Cedar Grove is remarkable primarily in its ordinariness. It stands as an example of how Christian churches can assess the needs of their communities and create meaningful relationships of solidarity that offer the possibility for social change and transformation. Churches and civil society groups that are involved in developing countercultural strategies for social change show people that viable alternatives to the dominant ideologies and power structures actually exist. While a theology of solidarity recognizes the importance of human contact and relationship, the strategies we need for large-scale social change will also require the development of ties of friendship and solidarity across member churches. Many faithful church members in the United States struggle daily trying to figure out what they can do to make a difference. We need to figure out how to link churches and church communities in the global North and the global South in meaningful ties that are not built on colonialism, paternalism, or resource transfer but that allow real bonds of Christian love and solidarity to be forged together. We also need to figure out how to link Christian communities with agencies, churches, and community groups in their own towns that are working on addressing the structural problems of poverty that face too many people. Soup kitchens, food pantries, and overnight shelters are a necessary aspect of responding to poverty in the world, but building meaningful relationships with people across boundaries and borders of difference offers deeper possibilities of transformation and justice in our communities. Working together to share effective strategies for social change, and imagining new ones, enables continued resistance to the dominant powers and presents possibilities for increased justice and sustainability in our world.

Notes

1. Grace Kao, "For All Creation," in *To Do Justice: A Guidebook for Progressive Christians*, ed. Rebecca Todd Peters and Elizabeth Hinson-Hasty (Louisville: Westminster John Knox, 2008), 99.

2. Ibid.

3. Several Christian ethicists have addressed significant issues of the working poor; see C. Melissa Snarr, *All You that Labor: Religion and Ethics in the Living Wage Movement* (New York: New York University Press, 2011); Ken Estey, *A New Protestant Labor Ethic at Work* (Eugene, OR: Wipf and Stock, 2011); Gloria H. Albrecht, *Hitting Home: Feminist Ethics, Women's Work, and the Betrayal of "Family Values,"* (New York: Continuum, 2002); Joan M. Martin, *More Than Chains and Toil: A Christian Work Ethic of Enslaved Women* (Louisville: Westminster John Knox, 2000); Pamela K. Brubaker, *Women Don't Count: The Challenge of Women's Poverty to Christian Ethics* (New York: Oxford University Press, 1994). See also Rebecca Todd Peters and Elizabeth Hinson-Hasty, *To Do*

Justice: A Guide for Progressive Christians (Louisville: Westminster John Knox, 2008), for a collection of essays designed to lead study groups in conversation about US social policies related to poverty.

4. All information about Sinapi Aba Trust and Alice Amoateng is taken from the Oikocredit International website: http://www.oikocredit.org/documents/pdf/projectsheet.pdf?&hit=no

5. This is informed by Paul Hawken's idea that "the promise of business is to increase the general well-being of humankind through service, a creative invention and ethical philosophy." See, Hawken, *The Ecology of Commerce* (New York: HarperCollins, 1993), 1.

6. M. Douglas Meeks, *God the Economist: The Doctrine of God and Political Economy* (Minneapolis: Fortress Press, 1989), 3.

7. Nancy Folbre, *The Invisible Heart: Economics and Family Values* (New York: The New Press, 2001).

8. TimeBanks, "Membership Directory," http://community.timebanks.org/.

9. For details, see Jon Tevlin, "To Ecuador, With Love," *Utne Reader*, July-August 2008.

10. Emily Kawano, "Crisis and Opportunity: The Emerging Solidarity Economy Movement," in *Solidarity Economy I: Building Alternatives for People and Planet*, ed. Emily Kawano, Thomas Neal Masterson, and Jonathan Teller-Elsberg (Amherst, MA: Center for Popular Economics, 2010), 17.

11. "Most relevant data," Mondragon Corporation, http://www.mondragon-corporation.com/language/en-US/ENG/Economic-Data/Most-relevant-data.aspx.

12. From remarks made by David Korten at the 2007 US Social Forum and transcribed in "Beyond Reform vs. Revolution: Economic Transformation in the U.S.," in *Solidarity Economy: Building Alternatives for People and Planet*, ed. Jenna Allard, Carl Davidson, and Julie Matthaei (Chicago: ChangeMaker, 2008), 103. Korten also serves on the board of BALLE.

13. BALLE website, http://bealocalist.org/about-us.

14. BALLE website, http://www.livingeconomies.org/aboutus/mission-and-principles.

15. Grace Hackney, interview with Caitlin Goodspeed, March 7, 2007.

16. Fred Bahnson, "A Garden Becomes A Protest: The Field at Anathoth," *Orion Magazine*, July/August 2007.

17. Fred Bahnson, "Compost for the Kingdom: An Experiment in Gardening," *Christian Century*, September 5, 2006.

18. Ibid.

19. Fred Bahnson, interview with Caitlin Goodspeed, March 19, 2007.

20. Grace Hackney, interview with Caitlin Goodspeed, March 7, 2007.

21. Grace Hackney, Pastoral Letter in Response to Recent Drug Violence, November 27, 2007, http://churches.nccumc.org/cedargrove/PG against drug violence.htm.

6

Conclusion: Hope for Tomorrow

When I teach environmental ethics, I often have my students do an exercise in which I tell them to imagine that it is the year 2075 and the environmental crisis has been resolved. I then tell them that they are a group of distinguished historians who have been brought together to outline a new textbook that will document the history of how our world got from its state of environmental crisis in the early decades of the twenty-first century to a healed and sustainable world in two generations.[1] Nine times out of ten, the groups start with a cataclysmic event—a nuclear war, an environmental event that destroys large segments of the population, or an infectious disease pandemic that likewise decimates the population. They then write a history in which sustainable agriculture and energy use are adopted universally and population rates are greatly reduced (often because so many people are killed).

This exercise offers some insight into the cultural barriers that must be overcome in order to redirect the attitudes and behaviors of people living in the first world. Most of these students consider themselves to be environmentalists; they readily accept that people in the first world are not living in a sustainable way, and yet the only hope they see for turning the situation around lies in catastrophe!

The task of challenging first-world Christians to think about issues of overconsumption, greed, and injustice is reminiscent of the words of Jeremiah.

> Thus says the Lord:
> Stand at the crossroads, and look,
> and ask for the ancient paths,
> where the good way lies; and walk in it,
> and find rest for your souls.
> But they said, "We will not walk in it."
>
> Therefore hear, O nations,
> and know, O congregation,

what will happen to them.
Hear, O earth; I am going to bring disaster on this people,
the fruit of their schemes,
because they have not given heed to my words;
and as for my teaching, they have rejected it. (Jeremiah 6:16, 18-19)

Recognizing the hermeneutical shift that is necessary to change the direction in which we are headed as a global community can bring despair. The assumptions of capitalism (growth, profit, and trade are a priori goods) and the lure of consumerism appear to have colonized the lifeworlds of the average American in ways that make it impossible to imagine or desire alternative ways of being.[2] This colonization functions like a drug, dulling the senses and keeping people floating just below consciousness. People are easier to manipulate that way. An obsessive preoccupation with shopping as entertainment fills closets and homes with useless gadgets, toys, and clothing that often goes unused. For too many people, consumption has become an addiction.

Like my students, most US Americans are unable to see our way past the present into a different future. Our addiction to "stuff" means that many people fear a loss of purchasing power will mean a corresponding loss of personal power or personal satisfaction or even self-worth. A new and different future in which people of means live in more sustainable ways is not yet seen as a social good, as a faithful and fulfilling experience of human life lived in covenant relationship with all God's creation. With Jeremiah (and my students), I sometimes fear that disaster is imminent. In fact, it is already present for many millions of our brothers and sisters around the world.

Yet as a Christian ethicist, I find hope in my tradition. In buying the field at Anathoth from his cousin during the middle of the siege, Jeremiah demonstrates that he is also an optimist. I take hope from the people in the first world who are choosing to live their lives in countercultural ways: from people in the Voluntary Simplicity Movement who offer an alternative vision of how to live simply in a consumer culture, from farmers who are committed to the sustainable practices of biodynamic farming in the face of the corporate machine that drives agriculture, from communities of citizens like the Zapatistas in Mexico who are standing up for their rights to self-determination, and from countless communities of faith across this country and around the world who are engaged in the work of social transformation and justice. It is a challenge to preach a gospel of solidarity to a public that might prefer a gospel of prosperity. It is much easier to interpret our economic and material accomplishments as blessings from God than to have to struggle with the theological question of why we have so much when others have so little. The theological question of trying to understand what "blessing" means in a world of vast inequality is also a deeply political question—as many theological questions often are.

The Social Gospel Movement that emerged in the late nineteenth century was born out of similar circumstances to the world in which we now live. Too many people were being exploited by the Industrial Revolution, and too few churches were involved in calling and working for change. In 1908, the Federal Council of Churches (the predecessor to the National Council of the Churches of Christ in the USA [NCC]) adopted a "Social Creed" at the instigation of the Social Gospelers. This creed and the work of many in the Social Gospel Movement prompted increased attention on the part of churches to the social problems of the world around them. In 2007, the NCC adopted a "Social Creed for the 21st Century" in recognition and celebration of the centenary of the 1908 creed. This new social creed offers an opportunity for pastors and church leaders to again find ways to address issues of social justice and social concern in local churches—in ways that go beyond the model of charity.[3]

While some pastors shy away from addressing economic or political issues from the pulpit, worried that they might ruffle the feathers of some of their flock, sociologist of religion Robert Wuthnow offers some hope regarding US American attitudes toward churches' involvement with contemporary social problems.[4] Wuthnow found in a study that 90 percent of Americans are at least fairly interested in social policies that would help the poor and legislation to protect the environment, and that 60 percent of people are quite interested in these issues.[5] In addition, wide majorities were fairly interested in overcoming discrimination against women in our society (87 percent); government policies to promote international peace (88 percent); achieving greater equality for racial and ethnic minorities in our society (86 percent); international human rights issues (81 percent); and the social responsibility of corporations (76 percent). Wuthnow comments that such a high level of interest in social issues among Americans indicates that church programs oriented toward these issues have the capacity to attract widespread support.[6]

Upon further study, Wuthnow found that when respondents were asked specifically if mainline Protestants should be more or less active in social issues, he found the following: 87 percent of respondents wanted churches to encourage people to do volunteer work; 82 percent thought churches should promote a greater sense of community; 78 percent thought churches should be more active in giving poor people a voice in public affairs; 77 percent wanted them to raise awareness about racial discrimination; 75 percent wanted them more involved in protecting the environment; and 70 percent thought churches should be making Americans more aware of hunger and poverty in other countries.[7] In addition to the moral imperative churches have to address these issues, it seems that people are ready and willing for churches to take a more activist role in addressing social problems in our world.

LIVING INTO HOPE

As first-world Christians seek to discern how to live into this new social reality of a globalized world that is fraught with injustice, inequality, and diminishing resources, it is important to listen carefully for where and how God is speaking in our world. As I listen for the voice of God speaking in the midst of the chaos, destruction, and injustice of our world, what I hear are the voices of my brothers and sisters from church communities across the two-thirds world who are speaking unambiguously through the ecumenical movement. The World Council of Churches and the World Communion of Reformed Churches (formerly World Alliance of Reformed Churches) have denounced as "sin" not only the structures and power of the global political economy as it is driven by neoliberal economic policies, but also the complicity and guilt of those of us who "consciously or unconsciously benefit from the current neoliberal economic global system."[8] Most churches in the first world have yet to grapple with the challenges that these documents and issues pose to our lifestyles and our dominant modes of being as people who disproportionately benefit from the capitalist political economies that shape globalization. From Brazil, Zimbabwe, the Philippines, and elsewhere in the two-thirds world, the voices of the ecumenical community call out, like Jeremiah, that the people have forsaken their God and are following false gods. But the question remains—how to speak God's word in ways that God's people can hear?

The temptation to relax and enjoy the privileges that first-world living offers can be very seductive. For many people of privilege who inhabit the first world, it is easy not to think about people in poverty; it is easy not to know what is happening with the WTO, the IMF, or the World Bank. In our consumer culture, it is easy to simply sit back and be entertained. However, God does not call people to a life of comfort, but a life of service.

As Christians struggle with the theological questions of privilege, blessing, and justice in a world of global poverty and inequality, we need to develop theologies that help us to change; theologies that reflect the power of *metanoia*; theologies that help make sense of the chaotic and unjust world in which we live. Liberation theologians have long argued that people who live on the margins of power and authority have a unique perspective that allows them to see things that people of privilege are blind to see.[9] The ethic of solidarity offered in this book is grounded in the idea that when people of privilege develop relationships with people who are different from them, it offers the possibility of helping first-world Christians develop a more adequate understanding of the world and the social problems that we face. Building relationships of solidarity with individuals and communities across lines of difference—be that across town or across the world—offers the possibility for *metanoia*, for first-world Christians to begin to see the world from new and different vantage points, vantage points that may disrupt what we think we know. The epistemological shifts that can arise from developing meaningful relationships of solidarity across lines of difference are a beacon of hope for those who are willing to risk embracing the challenge of seeing with new eyes.

I am proposing that we consider solidarity as a way of defining our obligation to the other as first-world Christians in a world where the forces of globalization privilege the few at the expense of our brothers and sisters across town and across the world. Solidarity represents an active relationship of support between two people or groups who are different from one another, in which one party stands with, supports, advocates for or otherwise generally acts as a partner to a person or group under duress. The starting point of this relationship of solidarity is mutuality.

While primarily a description of human relations and behavior, a theology of solidarity grows out of and is modeled on God's love and delight with the created world and God's unbounded mercy and care for creation. A theology of solidarity is not an intellectual exercise; it is primarily an ethic that can help people understand how to *live* in ways that honor God and God's creation in the contemporary world. Embracing solidarity as a moral norm means embracing an ethic of accountability that requires people not only to evaluate personal and collective actions in terms of how they impact our neighbors, but also to pursue concrete relationships with oppressed or marginalized communities that open us up to individual and collective transformation

This is no easy work. This is not the kind of Christian theology that celebrates the wealth and power of the United States and its allies or that sees our situation as the wealthiest country in the world as a reflection of God's blessing. This is a theology that asks us to account for the well-being of our brothers and sisters everywhere, without regard to their national heritage or even their religious affiliation (or lack thereof). This is an ethic of relationship and partnership that asks people of faith to examine our faith tradition as the foundation for asking how we should live in the world and what the world should look like.

IS THIS A THEOLOGY OF LIBERATION?

One of the foundational assumptions of liberation theology is that transformation and social change will only happen when people begin to work on structural change rather than trying to solve individual problems. This was the word that Sola spoke to me when she challenged me to use my education, my access, and my privilege as a first-world woman to challenge the powers of economic globalization at their source rather than to move to Nigeria to help a community of local people address their poverty. The issue is one of moving our practice from charity to social justice. While there is certainly a place for charity within the Christian tradition, the ethic of solidarity offered here focuses on the work of social justice as a necessary factor in changing the direction of our world toward a more just and peaceful community. Because privilege, wealth (relatively speaking), and comforts often blind people to the injustices of the world and how they are complicit in perpetuating them, the ethic of solidarity can be understood as a form of liberation theology for the privileged.[10]

Of course, engaging in liberation theology for the privileged is tricky business! After all, liberation theology arose in Latin America in contexts of extreme poverty and political oppression.[11] In the context of privilege in which many first-world Christians live, caution is in order when claiming one's work is a task of liberation. Too many first-world Christians display a dangerous tendency to spiritualize the meaning of "oppression" that can do very real violence to the insights of Latin American liberation theologians working in severe material deprivation. When poor people in Latin America read the story of the exodus, it makes sense for them to identify with the Hebrew slaves and to seek liberation from the bondages of poverty, illiteracy, political oppression, and violence that have marked the lives of many poor communities throughout the global South.[12] However, the theology of solidarity is directed toward those first-world Christians who, upon reading the story of the exodus, find they are more like the Egyptians than the Hebrew slaves. Like the Egyptians, many in the first world are the landowners, the taskmasters, or simply the ones who benefit from the exploitation of the labor of the workers. Reading Exodus with these eyes, the question for people with access to privilege becomes what God is calling them to do with the economic, political, and cultural power they have.

The theology of solidarity and the embodied ethic presented here are inspired by the methodological and theological insights of liberation theology. The development of an ethic of solidarity for first-world people grows out of the commitments of liberation theologians to the dignity and integrity of all God's creation, as well as the radical recognition of the moral agency and wisdom of people who have too often been discounted by the powers that be in society. Asking people of privilege to examine their wealth, status, and power as a prerequisite to entering into relationships of mutuality and solidarity with people across various lines of race, class, ability, nationality, and other forms of difference is a radically liberative step that challenges the dominant social and cultural powers. These powers thrive on the social isolation prevalent in contemporary society that prevents people from recognizing the many ways that they can work together to promote justice and the common good.

A theology for people of privilege in the first world will, necessarily, be different from a theology that helps people in the developing world make sense of the world around them. That is the point of understanding theology as *contextual*. This does not mean that the ultimate reality of the divine is different; just that people's experiences of the world necessarily shape their theology in distinct and meaningful ways.

The ethic of solidarity presented here is a vision of a different way of living that offers a glimpse of a better world. Some might even say it is a *new world*. While some might dismiss this as utopian,[13] it can also be read as a message of hope to the people who have asked over the years, "How can I live differently? What can we do to change the face of globalization in our world?" An ethic of solidarity is both a message of challenge and a word of hope. Embodying an ethic of solidarity is difficult work that requires commitment, discipline, and a willingness to risk. It is not an easy path, but one for those who are interested in struggling with the kind of challenging ethical questions raised by neoliberal globalization, economic inequality, and climate change. It is also not easy because some people we may want to build relationships with may not trust us or our motives. Given the history of racism and economic inequality, this is not surprising. Building relationships of solidarity will be a slow process that will require repeated evidence of the commitment of both parties. But living into an ethic of solidarity is not a tally of the particular relationships we might build, it is about the transformation of who we are and how we live. Embodying the four tasks of an ethic of solidarity—*metanoia*, honoring difference, accountability, and action—can set one on a new path for experiencing the world and for experiencing and knowing the divine.

As first-world Christians engage in a critical appraisal of their relative power and privilege, it is important to start by recognizing their own agency and dignity and the agency and dignity of people they hope to partner with. Developing relationships of solidarity across lines of difference is difficult and likely to be fraught with discomfort, misunderstanding, skepticism, and perhaps even hostility. In seeking to build these new relationships, the value of mutuality must be ever at the forefront of one's mind and heart. These relationships cannot be forced onto others but must arise out of contexts of trust and mutual vulnerability. First-world people of privilege may not have much experience with willingly making themselves vulnerable to others, but letting go of the need to be in charge or in control is one of the key challenges of relinquishing privilege.

ROOTED IN CHRISTIANITY, READY FOR DIALOGUE

An ethic of solidarity is intended to offer first-world Christians a pathway for living faithfully in an unjust world that is rooted in the values of the Christian tradition. While many Christians identify salvation as the focal point of Christian doctrine, the traditions of liberation and Reformed theology that ground this ethic equally emphasize the concrete realities of economic and social structures as well as the relationships between people and communities as the foundation of what it means to be a Christian. Thus while the vision offered here is grounded in Christian tradition and uses Christian stories and narratives to guide the way, it is not an exclusivist position. Because diverse religious communities and traditions share a common desire to help people understand themselves and the world, many of them ultimately share complementary values that could help to shape a better world. Diverse religious traditions also offer particular stories and traditions from which others can learn. An open heart and a willingness to listen to the stories, truths, and wisdom that abide in different religious traditions is a prerequisite for engaging as Christians in a multi-religious world in ways that embody mutuality and seek to establish relationships of solidarity—even across lines of religious difference.

Talking about how faith can inform the development of public policy is not the same thing as advocating theocracy. It does not require granting religious leaders political rule. In deliberative democracies, it is important to structure public conversations in ways that allow the insights from religious communities to become part of the discourse of civil society.

The complex nature of our world requires people of faith who understand their faith as relevant to the political and social structures of our world to engage in the difficult task of figuring out how to live in a world that is simultaneously secular and multi-religious. This is the final step of a meaningful Christian social ethic. Transparency about methodology, values, and commitments offers the possibility for people of different faith traditions and value systems to learn from one another and find the similarities and allegiances that exist between them. This kind of transparency can promote dialogue across lines of difference and facilitate communion and interreligious cooperation as people of faith work together to address the serious social problems that threaten our collective life. Religious communities and traditions represent significant sources of values and normative ethical guidance, and it is necessary for religious and spiritual people to work together to develop pathways for understanding each other and the common problems that the human community faces. Because an ethic of solidarity is not an exclusivist Christian theology, it offers the possibility for broad-based conversations across multiple lines of difference as people of faith seek ways of working together to build a world that is both sustainable and just.

Today, Christians in the first world are being called to account by our brothers and sisters from the global South for our participation in the systems and structures of empire and globalization that are impoverishing and exploiting their lives, their families, and their communities. As people of faith, as brothers and sisters in Christ, we are called to listen to their voices, their stories, and their experiences—and to examine our own lives in the process. Let history not convict us of being naïvely complicit in an unjust social system that is economically advantageous to us at the expense of the exploitation and dehumanization of other human beings. Seeking transformation toward justice is part of our responsibility to live faithfully into our covenant relationship with God and all of God's creation.

Notes

1. This exercise is modified from a popular education website that suggests a similar exercise called "Backcasting a Solution": http://www.psicopolis.com/GruppoNew/esercitazfor.htm.

2. Jurgen Habermas, *The Theory of Communicative Action, Volume 2: Lifeworld and System: A Critique of Functionalist Reason*, trans. Thomas McCarthy (Boston: Beacon, 1987).

3. See Rebecca Todd Peters and Elizabeth Hinson-Hasty, *To Do Justice: A Guide for Progressive Christians*, Louisville: Westminster John Knox, 2008 for an introduction to the 21st Century Social Creed and study chapters on many of the issues it raises.

4. Robert Wuthnow, "Beyond Quiet Influence? Possibilities for the Protestant Mainline," in *Quiet Hand of God: Faith-Based Activism and the Public Role of Mainline Protestantism*, ed. Robert Wuthnow and John H. Evans (Berkeley: University of California Press, 2002), 383.

5. Ibid., 384.

6. Ibid.

7. Ibid., 386.

8. WARC statement, "Covenanting for Justice in the Economy and the Earth," article 34, and Commission for Justice, Peace and Creation, "Alternative Globalization Addressing Peoples and Earth—AGAPE document" (World Council of Churches, 2006).

9. This is known as the "epistemological privilege of the poor," which means that there is particular knowledge that comes from the vantage point of people on the underside of history. From their perspective, the poor and marginalized are able to ask critical questions about how we know what we know that unveil abuses of power and influence, exploitation, and other examples of injustice that are often invisible to people with privilege and power.

10. Just as the oppressed need to be liberated from oppression, those who participate in the oppression of others need to be liberated from the shackles that bind them. While the suffering of the oppressor is never equivalent to that of the oppressed, oppression destroys the humanity of the oppressor as surely as it does the oppressed. Many first-world theologians have discussed the need for the liberation of the oppressors; see Jürgen Moltmann with M. Douglas Meeks, "The Liberation of Oppressors," *Christianity and Crisis* 38, no. 20 (Dec. 25, 1978), 310–17 for an early discussion of this question. See Glenn R. Bucher, "Toward a Liberation Theology for the 'Oppressor,'" *Journal of the American Academy of Religion* 44, no. 3 (1976), 517–34 for an early analysis of responses to liberation theology. See Mary Elizabeth Hobgood, *Dismantling Privilege: An Ethics of Accountability* (Cleveland: Pilgrim, 2000) for a well-developed liberation ethic for oppressors.

11. Curt Cadorette, Marie Giblin, Marilyn J. Legge, and Mary H. Snyder, *Liberation Theology: An Introductory Reader* (Maryknoll, NY: Orbis, 1997).

12. There are those in the first world who also experience the violence of poverty, disenfranchisement, prejudice, and oppression—none more so than the original inhabitants of the neo-Europes and colonies, First Nations people, Native Americans, Aborigines and other indigenous groups. The crafting of liberation theology for oppressed groups is of vital importance; that work is being done, most appropriately, by people who are more clearly identified with those particular communities. The development of an ethic of solidarity for first-world Christians is, in itself, a reflection of solidarity, as it is intended to help guide more privileged Christians to think deeply and critically about the task of human community, loving neighbor (mutuality), and embodying the call to "do justice."

13. Liberation theologians have often been criticized by Christian realists for promoting utopian ideas that do not take into consideration the reality of human sin and imperfection. Karen Lebacqz, *Six Theories of Justice: Perspectives from Philosophical and Theological Ethics* (Minneapolis: Augsburg Fortress, 1986), 110.

Bibliography

Albrecht, Gloria H. *Hitting Home: Feminist Ethics, Women's Work, and the Betrayal of "Family Values."* New York: Continuum, 2002.

Alexander, Michelle. *The New Jim Crow: Mass Incarceration in an Age of Colorblindness.* New York: The New Press, 2010.

Andolsen, Barbara Hilkert, Christine E. Gudorf, and Mary. D. Pellauer, eds. *Women's Consciousness, Women's Conscience: A Reader in Feminist Ethics.* San Francisco: Harper & Row, 1985.

Appiah, Kwame Anthony. *Cosmopolitanism: Ethics in a World of Strangers.* New York: W. W. Norton, 2006.

Atherton, John. *Transfiguring Capitalism: An Enquiry into Religion and Global Change.* London: SCM, 2008.

———, and Hannah Skinner, eds. *Through the Eye of a Needle: Theological Conversations Over Political Economy.* Petersborough, UK: Epworth, 2007.

Bahnson, Fred. "A Garden Becomes A Protest: The Field at Anathoth." *Orion Magazine,* July/August 2007.

———. "Compost for the Kingdom: An Experiment in Gardening." *Christian Century,* September 5, 2006.

———. Interview with Caitlin Goodspeed. March 19, 2007.

Barndt, Joseph. *Understanding and Dismantling Racism: The Twenty-First Century Challenge to White America.* Minneapolis: Fortress Press, 2007.

Bayertz, Kurt, ed. *Solidarity.* Dordrecht, The Netherlands: Kluwer Academic, 1999.

Berger, Joseph. "100 Years Later, the Roll of the Dead in a Factory Fire Is Complete." *New York Times,* February 20, 2011.

Bernstein, Jared, Lawrence Mishel, and Sylvia A. Allegretto. *State of Working America 2006/2007.* New York: Cornell University, 2007.

Berquist, Jon L. "Resistance and Accommodation in the Roman Empire." In *In The Shadow of the Empire: Reclaiming the Bible as a History of Faithful Resistance,* edited by Richard A. Horsley. Louisville: Westminster John Knox, 2008.

Brown, Melissa S., and Patrick M. Rooney. "Giving Following a Crisis: An Historical Analysis." Center on Philanthropy at Indiana University. Released

January 2010, http://www.philanthropy.iupui.edu/Research/Giving/Crisis%20Giving%20paper%203-24-031.pdf.

Brubaker, Pamela K. *Women Don't Count: The Challenge of Women's Poverty to Christian Ethics*. New York: Oxford University Press, 1994.

———, and Rogate Mshana, eds. *Justice Not Greed*. Geneva: World Council of Churches, 2010.

Bucher, Glenn R. "Toward a Liberation Theology for the 'Opressor,'" *Journal of the American Academy of Religion* 44, no. 3 (1976): 517–34.

Cadorette, Curt, et al. *Liberation Theology: An Introductory Reader*. Maryknoll, NY: Orbis, 1997.

Cannon, Katie. *Katie's Canon: Womanism and the Soul of the Black Community*. New York: Continuum, 1995.

Cassidy, Laurie M., and Alex Mikulich, eds. *Interrupting White Privilege: Catholic Theologians Break the Silence*. Maryknoll, NY: Orbis, 2007.

Caufield, Catherine. *Masters of Illusion: The World Bank and Poverty of Nations*. New York: Henry Holt, 1996.

Center for Disease Control and Prevention. *National Vital Statistics Report* 59, no. 4 (2011): 6.

Center on Philanthropy at Indiana University. "Disaster Giving Timeline." Ongoing research, Indiana University, 2011. http://www.philanthropy.iupui.edu/disaster-giving.

"Corporate Profile 2010 (Annual Report)." Mondragon Corporation. http://www.mondragon-corporation.com/mcc_dotnetnuke/Portals/0/documentos/eng/Corporative-Profile/Corporative-Profile.html.

"Covenanting for Justice in the Economy and the Earth (Accra Confession)." 24th General Council of the World Alliance of Reformed Churches, Accra, Ghana, 2004.

Davis, David Brion. *Inhuman Bondage: The Rise and Fall of Slavery in the New World*. New York: Oxford, 2006.

de la Torre, Miguel. "For Immigrants." In *To Do Justice: A Guide for Progressive Christians*, edited by Rebecca Todd Peters and Elizabeth Hinson-Hasty, 73–84. Louisville: Westminster John Knox, 2008.

DeNavas-Walt, Carmen, Bernadetta D. Proctor, and Jessica C. Smith. *Income, Poverty, and Health Insurance Coverage in the United States: 2010*. Washington DC: U.S. Census Bureau, September 2011.

Doran, Kevin P. *Solidarity: A Synthesis of Personalism and Communalism in the Thought of Karol Wojtyla/Pope John Paul II*. New York: Peter Lang, 1996.

Dorrien, Gary. *Soul in Society: The Making and Renewal of Social Christianity.* Minneapolis: Fortress Press, 1995.

Dube, Musa. "Postcoloniality, Feminist Spaces, and Religion." In *Postcolonialism, Feminism, and Religious Discourse,* edited by Laura Donaldson and Kwok Pui-lan, 100–122. New York: Routledge, 2002.

Duchrow, Ulrich, and Franz J. Hinkelammert. *Property for People, Not for Profit: Alternatives to the Global Tyranny of Capital.* London: Zed Books, in association with The Catholic Institute for International Relations, 2004.

Durkheim, Émile. *The Division of Labor in Society.* Translated by W.D. Halls. 1933. Reprint, New York: Free Press, 1997.

Ellsberg, Robert. Introduction to *The Logic of Solidarity: Commentaries on Pope John II's Encyclical "On Social Concern."* Edited by Gregory Baum and Robert Ellsberg. Maryknoll, NY: Orbis, 1989.

Estey, Ken. *A New Protestant Labor Ethic at Work.* Eugene, OR: Wipf & Stock, 2011.

Eubanks, Ralph, and Mark Anthony Neal. "The 'Post-Racial' Conversation, One Year In." Interview by Rebecca Roberts. *Talk of the Nation.* National Public Radio, January 18, 2010.

Folbre, Nancy. *The Invisible Heart: Economics and Family Values.* New York: The New Press, 2001.

Frankenberg, Ruth. *White Women, Race Matters: The Social Construction of Whiteness.* Minneapolis: University of Minnesota Press, 1993.

Friere, Paulo. *Pedagogy of the Oppressed.* Translated by Myra Bergman Ramos. New York: Continuum, 2000.

Glick, Reuven, and Kevin J. Lansing. "Consumers and the Economy, Part I: Household Credit and Personal Saving." *FRBSF (Federal Reserve Bank San Francisco) Economic Letter.* January 10, 2011.

Goudzwaard, Bob, Mark Vander Vennen, and David Van Heemst. *Hope in Troubled Times: A New Vision for Confronting Global Crises.* Grand Rapids: Baker Academic, 2007.

Grassi, Joseph A. *Informing the Future: Social Justice in the New Testament.* Mahwah, NJ: Paulist, 2003.

Greider, William. *One World, Ready or Not: The Manic Logic of Global Capitalism.* New York: Simon & Schuster, 1997.

Gutiérrez, Gustavo. *The Density of the Present: Selected Writings.* Maryknoll, NY: Orbis, 1999.

———. *A Theology of Liberation: History, Politics and Salvation.* Maryknoll, NY: Orbis, 1973.

Habermas, Jurgen. *The Structural Transformation of the Public Spehere: An Inquiry into a Category of Bourgeois Society.* 1962. Translated by Thomas Burger with the assistance of Frederick Lawrence. Cambridge: The MIT Press, 1989.

———. *The Theory of Communicative Action, Volume Two: Lifeworld and System: A Critique of Functionalist Reason.* 1981. Translated by Thomas McCarthy. Boston: Beacon, 1989.

Hackney, Grace. Interview by Caitlin Goodspeed. March 7, 2007.

———. "Pastoral Letter in Response to Recent Drug Violence." November 27, 2007, http://churches.nccumc.org/cedargrove/PG against drug violence.htm.

Haidt, Jonathan. "The Emotional Dog and Its Rational Tail: A Social Intuitionist Approach to Moral Judgment." *Psychological Review* 108, no. 4 (2001): 814–34.

———. *The Happiness Hypothesis: Finding Modern Truth in Ancient Wisdom.* New York: Basic, 2006.

Hall, Holly, and Debra E. Blum. "Coming on Strong." *Chronicle of Philanthropy* 18, no. 18 (June 29, 2006): 23–27.

Harrison, Beverly Wildung. *Our Right To Choose: Toward a New Ethic of Abortion.* Boston: Beacon, 1983.

———. "Theological Reflection in the Struggle for Liberation." In *Making the Connections: Essays in Feminist Social Ethics,* edited by Carol S. Robb, 235–66. Boston: Beacon, 1985.

Harvey, David. *A Brief History of Neoliberalism.* New York: Oxford, 2005.

Harvey, Jennifer, Karin A. Case, and Robin Hawley Gorsline, eds. *Disrupting White Supremacy from Within: White People On What We Need To Do.* Cleveland, OH: Pilgrim, 2004.

———. *Whiteness and Morality: Pursuing Racial Justice through Reparations and Sovereignty.* New York: Palgrave Macmillan, 2007.

Hawken, Paul. *The Ecology of Commerce.* New York: HarperCollins, 1993.

Hayes, Christopher. "In Search of Solidarity." *In These Times,* February 3, 2006. http://www.inthesetimes.com/main/print/2484/.

Hilfiker, David. *Urban Injustice: How Ghettos Happen.* New York: Seven Stories, 2002.

Hobgood, Mary Elizabeth. *Dismantling Privilege: An Ethics of Accountability.* Cleveland: Pilgrim, 2000.

———. "Solidarity and the Accountability of Academic Feminists and Church Activists to Typical (World-Majority) Women," *Journal of Feminist Studies in Religion* 20, no. 2 (2004): 137–65.

————. "Solidarity and the Accountability of Academic Feminists and Church Activists to Typical (World-Majority) Women." *Journal of Feminist Studies in Religion* 20, no. 2 (2004): 137–65.

Horkheimer, Max. "Traditional and Critical Theory." In *Critical Theory: Selected Essays,* translated by Matthew J. O'Connell, 188–243. New York: Continuum, 2002.

Hough, Joseph C., Jr. "Christian Social Ethics as Advocacy," *Journal of Religious Ethics* 5, no. 1 (1997): 115–33.

Isasi-Díaz, Ada María. "Solidarity: Love of Neighbor in the 1980s." In *Feminist Theological Ethics: A Reader,* edited by Lois K. Daly, 77–87. Louisville: Westminster John Knox, 1994.

Jacobs, Jill. *There Shall Be No Needy: Pursuing Social Justice through Jewish Law and Tradition.* Woodstock, VT: Jewish Lights, 2009.

Jacobsen, Dennis A. *Doing Justice: Congregations and Community Organizing.* Minneapolis: Fortress Press, 2001.

John XXIII. *Mater et Magistra.* Encyclical letter on Christianity and social progress. Vatican City: 1961.

John Paul II. *Sollicitudo Rei Socialis.* Encyclical letter on social concern. Vatican City: 1987.

Johnson, Victoria, and Andrew Simms. *Chinadependence: The Second UK Interdependence Report.* London: New Economics Foundation, 2007.

Kao, Grace. "For All Creation." In *To Do Justice: A Guidebook for Progressive Christians,* edited by Rebecca Todd Peters and Elizabeth Hinson-Hasty, 73–84. Louisville: Westminster John Knox, 2008.

Kautsky, Karl. *The Class Struggle (Erfurt Program).* 1892. Translated by William E. Bohn. Chicago: Charles H. Kerr, 1910.

Kawano, Emily. "Crisis and Opportunity: The Emerging Solidarity Economy Movement." In *Solidarity Economy I: Building Alternatives for People and Planet,* edited by Emily Kawano, Thomas Neal Masterson, and Jonathan Teller-Elsberg, 11–24. Amherst, MA: Center for Popular Economics, 2010.

Kendall, Frances E. *Understanding White Privilege: Creating Pathways to Authentic Relationships Across Race.* New York: Routledge, Taylor and Francis Group, 2006.

King, Martin Luther, Jr. "Address at the Fourth Annual Institute on Nonviolence and Social Change at Bethel Baptist Church, December 3, 1959." In *The Papers of Martin Luther King, Jr, Volume 5: Threshold of a New Decade, January 1959–December 1960,* edited by Clayborne Carson, 333–43. Los Angeles: University of California Press, 2005.

Korgen, Jeffry Odell. *Solidarity Will Transform the World: Stories of Hope from Catholic Relief Services.* Maryknoll, NY: Orbis, 2007.

Korten, David, Julie Matthaei, Emily Kawano, Dan Swinney, Germai Medhanie, and Stephen Healy. "Beyond Reform vs. Revolution: Economic Transformation in the U.S., A Roundtable Discussion." In *Solidarity Economy: Building Alternatives for People and Planet,* edited by Jenna Allard, Carl Davidson, and Julie Matthaei, 100–122. Chicago: ChangeMaker Publications, 2008.

Kristof, Nicolas D. "Racism Without Racists." *New York Times,* October 4, 2008.

Latin American Bishops, "Poverty of the Church." *Conference of Latin American Bishops.* Medellin, Colombia, September 6, 1968.

Lebacqz, Karen. *Six Theories of Justice: Perspectives from Philosophical and Theological Ethics.* Minneapolis: Augsburg Fortress, 1986.

Liedman, Sven-Eric. "Solidarity." Translated by Ken Schubert. *Eurozine.* 2002.

Long, Edward LeRoy. *To Liberate and Redeem: Moral Reflections on the Biblical Narrative.* Cleveland: Pilgrim, 1996.

Long, Stephen D., Nancy Ruth Fox, and Tripp York. *Calculated Futures: Theology, Ethics, and Economics.* Waco, TX: Baylor University Press, 2007.

Louw, J. P., and Eugene A. Nida, eds. *Greek-English Lexicon of the New Testament: Based on Semantic Domains.* 2nd ed. 2 vols. New York: United Bible Societies, 1989.

Malchow, Bruce V. *Social Justice in the Hebrew Bible.* Collegeville, MN: Liturgical, 1996.

Martin, Joan M. *More Than Chains and Toil: A Christian Work Ethic of Enslaved Women.* Louisville: Westminster John Knox, 2000.

Matthews, Sally. "Inherited or Earned Advantage?" *Mail and Guardian,* September 12, 2011.

McCann, Dennis. *Christian Realism and Liberation Theology: Practical Theologies in Creative Conflict.* Maryknoll, NY: Orbis, 1981.

McFague, Sallie. *Metaphorical Theology: Models of God in Religious Language.* Minneapolis: Fortress Press, 1982.

———. *Models of God: Theology for an Ecological, Nuclear Age.* Philadelphia: Fortress Press, 1987.

McGinnis, James. *Solidarity with the People of Nicaragua.* Maryknoll, NY: Orbis, 1985.

McIntosh, Peggy. "White Privilege and Male Privilege: A Personal Account of Coming to See Correspondences Through Work in Women's Studies."

Working paper #189, Wellesley College Center for Research on Women, Wellesley, MA, 1988.

———. "White Privilege: Unpacking the Invisible Knapsack." In *Race, Class, and Gender in the United States*. Edited by Paula S. Rothenberg, 188–92. 6th ed. New York: Worth, 2004.

Meadows, Donella, Jorgen Randers, and Dennis Meadows. *Limits to Growth: The 30-Year Update*. White River Junction, VT: Chelsea Green, 2004.

Meeks, M. Douglas. *God the Economist: The Doctrine of God and Political Economy*. Minneapolis: Fortress Press, 1989.

Moltmann, Jürgen, with M. Douglas Meeks. "The Liberation of Oppressors." *Christianity and Crisis* 38, no. 20 (Dec. 25, 1978): 310–17.

Min, Anselm. *The Solidarity of Others in a Divided World: A Postmodern Theology after Postmodernism*. New York: T & T Clark, 2004.

Mondragon Corporation. "Most relevant data." Mondragon Economic Data. http://www.mondragon-corporation.com/language/en-US/ENG/Economic-Data/Most-relevant-data.aspx.

Munoz-Dardé, Véronique. "Fraternity and Justice." In *Solidarity*, edited by Kurt Bayertz, 81–99. Dordrecht, The Netherlands: Kluwer Academic, 1999.

Myers, Jacob M. *Ezra-Nehemiah,* Anchor Yale Bible Commentaries. New Haven: Yale University Press, 1995.

"A Nation Challenged: Choice of Words; Mission Title May Change." *New York Times*, September 21, 2001.

Nelson, Julie A. *Economics for Humans*. Chicago: The University of Chicago Press, 2006.

"New York Times Poll: Class Project." March 13–14, 2005, http://www.nytimes.com/packages/html/national/20050515_CLASS_GRAPHIC/index_04.html.

O'Connor, June. "On Doing Religious Ethics," in *Women's Consciousness, Women's Conscience,* edited by Barbara Hilkert Andolsen, Christine E. Gudorf, and Mary D. Pellauer. Minneapolis: Winston, 1985.

Oxfam International. "Scarlett Johansson Designs a Handbag for Haiti." Oxfam International press release. Last modified February 4, 2010. http://www.oxfam.org/en/pressroom/pressrelease/2010-02-04/scarlett-johansson-designs-handbag-haiti.

Paris, Peter. *The Brueggemann and Kulenkamp Lectures for Continuing Education*. Unpublished lecture, Eden Theological Seminary, St. Louis, Missouri, April 1–2, 2008.

Parker, Paul Plenge, ed. *Standing with the Poor: Theological Reflections on Economic Reality.* Cleveland: Pilgrim, 1992.

Parry, Marc. "Jonathan Haidt Decodes the Tribal Psychology of Politics." *Chronicle of Higher Education,* January 29, 2012, http://chronicle.com/article/Jonathan-Haidt-Decodes-the/130453/.

Paul VI. *Popularum Progessio.* Encyclical letter on the development of peoples. Vatican City: 1967.

Peitz, Darlene Ann. *Solidarity as Hermeneutic: A Revisionist Reading of the Theology of Walter Rauschenbusch.* New York: Peter Lang, 1992.

Peralta, Athena K. *A Caring Economy: A Feminist Contribution to Alternatives to Globalisation Adressing People and Earth.* Geneva: World Council of Churches, 2005.

Peters, Rebecca Todd. "Economic Justice Requires More than the Kindness of Strangers." In *Global Neighbors: Christian Faith and Moral Obligation in Today's Economy,* edited by Douglas A. Hicks and Mark Valeri. Grand Rapids: Eerdmans, 2008.

———. *In Search of the Good Life: The Ethics of Globalization.* New York: Continuum, 2004.

———, and Elizabeth Hinson-Hasty. *To Do Justice: A Guide for Progressive Christians.* Louisville: Westminster John Knox, 2008.

Pope, Stephen J., ed. *Hope and Solidarity: Jon Sobrino's Challenge to Christian Theology.* Maryknoll, NY: Orbis, 2008.

Porter, Katherine, ed. *Broke: How Debt Bankrupts the Middle Class.* Stanford: Stanford University Press, 2012.

Poverty, Wealth and Ecology. Calgary, Alberta: World Council of Churches, 2012.

Preston, Ronald. "Middle Axioms." In *Dictionary of Christian Ethics,* edited by James F. Childress and John Macquarrie. Philadelphia: Westminster, 1986.

Princen, Thomas. "Consumption and its Externalities: Where Economy Meets Ecology." In *Confronting Consumption,* edited by Thomas Princen, Michael Maniates, and Ken Conca, 1–19. Boston: MIT, 2002.

Rawls, John. *A Theory of Justice.* Cambridge: Harvard University Press, 1971.

Rich, Bruce. *Mortgaging the Earth: The World Bank, Environmental Impoverishment, and the Crisis of Development.* Boston: Beacon, 1994.

Rieger, Joerg. *No Rising Tide: Theology, Economics, and the Future.* Minneapolis: Fortress Press, 2009.

———. *Remember the Poor: The Challenge to Theology in the Twenty-First Century.* Harrisburg, PA: Trinity Press International, 1998.

Robb, Carol S. "Rational Man and Feminist Economists on Welfare Reform." In *Welfare Policy: Feminist Critiques*, edited by Elizabeth M. Bounds, Pamela K. Brubaker, and Mary E. Hobgood, 77–94, Cleveland: Pilgrim, 1999.

Sachs, Jeffrey D. *The End of Poverty: Economic Possibilities for our Time*. New York: Penguin Books, 2005.

Sacks, Jonathan. *The Dignity of Difference: How to Avoid the Clash of Civilizations*. London: Continuum, 2002.

Sawyer, Mary R. *The Church on the Margins: Living Christian Communities*. New York: Continuum, 2003.

Scholz, Sally J. *Political Solidarity*. University Park: Pennsylvania State University Press, 2008.

Segrest, Mab. *Memoir of a Race Traitor*. Boston: South End, 1994.

Smith, Adam. *Theory of Moral Sentiments*. 1759. Edited by D. D. Raphael and A. L. Macfie. 1976. Reprint, Indianapolis: Liberty Fund, 1982.

———. *An Inquiry into the Nature and Causes of the Wealth of Nations*. Vols. 1 and II. 1775. Edited by R. H. Campbell and A.S. Skinner. 1979. Reprint, Indianapolis: Liberty Fund, 1981.

Smith, Lillian. *Killers of the Dream: Revised and Enlarged*. New York: W. W. Norton, 1949.

Snarr, Melissa. *All You that Labor: Religion and Ethics in the Living Wage Movement*. New York: New York University Press, 2011.

Sobrino, Jon, and Juan Hernandez Pico. *Theology of Christian Solidarity*. Maryknoll, NY: Orbis, 1985.

Sparr, Pamela, ed. *Mortgaging Women's Lives: Feminist Critiques of Structural Adjustment*. London: Zed, 1994.

Stiglitz, Joseph E. *Globalization and Its Discontents*. New York: W. W. Norton, 2002.

———. "Student Debt and the Crushing of the American Dream". *New York Times*, Opinionator, May 12, 2013.

Stjernø, Steinar. *Solidarity in Europe: The History of an Idea*. Cambridge: Cambridge University Press, 2004.

Sturm, Douglas. *Solidarity and Suffering: Towards a Politics of Relationality*. Albany: State University of New York, 1998.

Taylor, Michael. *Christianity, Poverty and Wealth: The Findings of 'Project 21.'* Geneva: World Council of Churches, 2003.

Taylor, Paul, Richard Fry, and Rakesh Kochar. "Wealth Gaps Rise to Record Highs Between Whites, Blacks, Hispanics." In *Social and Demographic Trends*. Washington, DC: Pew Research Center, July 26, 2011.

http://pewsocialtrends.org/files/2011/07/SDT-Wealth-Report_7-26-11_FINAL.pdf.

Tevlin, Jon. "To Ecuador, With Love." *Utne Reader*, July–August 2008.

Thandeka. *Learning to Be White: Money, Race, and God in America*. New York: Continuum, 1999.

Theological Reflection on Accompaniment: Ecumenical Accompaniment Programme in Palestine and Israel. Geneva: World Council of Churches, 2005.

TimeBanks. "Membership Directory," http://community.timebanks.org/.

Timmerman, Kelsey. *Where Am I Wearing?: A Global Tour to the Countries, Factories, and People that Make Our Clothes*. Hoboken, NJ: John Wiley, 2009.

Tinker, George E. *Missionary Conquest: The Gospel and Native American Cultural Genocide*. Minneapolis: Fortress Press, 1993.

Toten, Suzanne C. *Justice Education: From Service to Solidarity*. Milwaukee, WI: Marquette University Press, 2006.

Townes, Emilie M. "From Mammy to Welfare Queen: Images of Black Women in Public Policy Formation." In *Beyond Slavery: Overcoming Its Religious and Sexual Legacies*, edited by Bernadette J. Brooten, 61–74. New York: Palgrave, 2010.

Trible, Phyllis. *God and the Rhetoric of Sexuality*. Philadelphia: Fortress Press, 1978.

United Nations Development Program. *The Human Development Report*, 1998. http://hdr.undp.org/en/reports/global/hdr1998.

United States Census Bureau. "U.S. Census Bureau Economic Indicators." July 1, 2011. http://www.census.gov/#.

———. "Table 720. Family Net Worth—Mean and Median Net Worth in Constant (2007) Dollars by Selected Family Characteristics: 1998–2007." In *Statistical Abstract of the United States: 2011*. http://www.census.gov/prod/2011pubs/11statab/income.pdf.

"US Census Bureau Economic Indicatiors," http://www.census.gov/cgi-bin/briefroom/BriefRm.

Van Til, Kent A. *Less Than Two Dollars a Day: a Christian View of World Poverty and the Free Market*. Grand Rapids: Eerdmans, 2007.

Venetoulis, Jason, Dahlia Chazan, and Christopher Gaudet. *Ecological Footprint of Nations 2004*. Oakland, CA: Redefining Progress, 2004. http://www.globalchange.umich.edu/globalchange2/current/labs/ecofoot/footprintnations2004.pdf

Ventura, Patricia. *Neoliberal Culture: Living with American Neoliberalism*. London: Ashgate, 2012.

Welch, Sharon D. *A Feminist Ethic of Risk*. Minneapolis: Fortress Press, 1990.

———. *Communities of Resistance and Solidarity: A Feminist Theology of Liberation*. Maryknoll, NY: Orbis, 1985.

White House Office of Management and Budget, *Historical Tables: Table 1.1—Summary of Receipts, Outlays, and Surpluses or Deficits: 1789–2018*.

World Bank. *World Development Indicators, 2008*. Washington, DC: Development Data Group, 2008. http://data.worldbank.org/sites/default/files/wdi08.pdf.

World Bank Press. "World Bank Sees Progress Against Extreme Poverty, But Flags Vulnerabilities." World Bank Press release, February 29, 2012.

World Council of Churches. "Alternative Globalization Addressing People and the Earth (AGAPE)." Geneva: WCC Publishing, 2006.

World Health Organization. "Maternal mortality: helping women off the road to death." *WHO Chronicle* 40, no. 5 (1986): 175–83.

World Wildlife Fund. *Living Planet Report 2006*. Gland, Switzerland: World Wildlife Fund, 2006.

The Worldwatch Institute. *State of the World 2004*. New York: W. W. Norton, 2004.

Wuthnow, Robert, and John H. Evans, eds. *The Quiet Hand of God: Faith-Based Activism and the Public Role of Mainline Protestantism*. Berkeley: University of California Press, 2002.

Index

CPSIA information can be obtained
at www.ICGtesting.com
Printed in the USA
FFOW03n1641190817
38956FF